SQUARING OFF

SQUARING OFF

MAILER VS. BALDWIN

BY W.J. WEATHERBY

 MASON/CHARTER   NEW YORK 1977

Library of Congress Cataloging in Publication Data

Weatherby, William J   Squaring off.
  1. Mailer, Norman—Biography. 2. Baldwin, James,
1924–   —Biography. 3. Authors, American—20th
century—Bibliography. I. Title.
PS129.W4   813'.5'4 [B]   76-53559
ISBN 0-88405-449-7

For
Kathleen Weatherby, Thomas and Sheila Weatherby, James
Monroe Parker, Drucilla Crosby Parker, Norman Folsom,
Ernestine Lee, Melva Franklin, Edith Whiteman

For my editor, Margaret B. Parkinson

and in memory of Gertie Wood, who appears in this book but
didn't live to read it.

INTRODUCTION

Cain and Abel, Jekyll and Hyde, Holmes and Watson, even Sartre and Camus . . . but why Mailer and Baldwin?

Because they are reverse sides of the same coin, representative figures of the sixties, when blacks and whites were struggling creatively to understand each other.

Langston Hughes once told me, "The story of America still cannot be told through either a white or a black figure. No *one* figure is representative, not even a Lincoln. You always have to find The Other, the other side of the coin. You have to look for a strange duality of human experience—a John Kennedy *and* a Martin Luther King—to tell the story of any period, but particularly the tumultuous sixties, when so much is changing."

When I first met Norman Mailer and James Baldwin at the start of that decade, they hadn't yet been made into super-stars and they didn't seem to have much in common except that they were both writers, both New Yorkers, and both about the same age. Mailer was pursuing experiences—although in an extreme form—that were typical of his generation of whites. Baldwin was caught up in the black renascence and the beginnings of the latest civil rights movement, a very representative black experience.

Yet the more I saw of both men over the next few years—interviewing Mailer, encountering him as an aggressive host, as an equally aggressive guest; seeing Baldwin attacking whites in

1

groups and yet loving individuals, relaxing in the bosom of his family—the two men did begin to seem strangely related, like Langston Hughes' opposite sides of the same coin. They were both involved in a common quest in public even though in different directions and styles, white and black. It was a search on the national stage, beneath the media's spotlights—a search that mirrored a great many other similar but private searches conducted by unknown individuals. Mailer and Baldwin were frontline voyagers for a lot of fellow Americans.

Both men obviously felt some subtle kind of connection. They studied each other with intense curiosity, the way a boxer studies an opponent. In those militant times, their different color was a challenge—a challenge they accepted more readily than most of their contemporaries. They wrote about each other several times. And their instincts were right: they had much more in common than other writers of their age. But everything in one tended to be reversed in the other; each was searching for what the other had already found.

Mailer said once, referring to marriage, that you had to fight before you could possibly understand another person; and Baldwin has shown a similar faith in conflict as a means to a close relationship. Over the ten years I observed them, they seemed to be involved in a conflict with each other, forever about to climb into some intellectual ring or to stage a symbolic confrontation at High Noon. And the outcome of their Big Fight—white Aquarius versus black Leo—was obviously going to be as important to a great many other people as to themselves . . . if it ever took place! What happened on the way to that ever-threatening High Noon is the story of this book.

Writing about living people is a responsibility, but I have used Mailer's and Baldwin's own books as my guide, allowing myself—as they have done—to be true to my experience even when it might seem unfriendly or unfair. I have enjoyed the same freedom they have to speculate about the relationship between a writer's life and his work. I have quoted conversations I noted at the time or in my diary immediately afterward,

2

but I have omitted them when all I had to depend on was my memory, for a trained reporter's memory can play tricks like anyone else's when you are writing in the seventies about the faraway sixties.

1

James Baldwin wasn't famous when I first met him. Nor was he rich. He had made it from Harlem poverty to more of the same in Europe, nine years of Europe, and then he had returned to live for the time being in the Village, managing somehow to survive off his writing. That was when I met him, in the summer of 1959.

Tennessee Williams provided my introduction. I had sat for an afternoon in Williams' disheveled fifth-floor apartment on the East side of New York, listening to him tell of his anguish over the recent Broadway production of his latest play, *Sweet Bird of Youth.* A large Spanish parrot perched on my shoulder and inspected one of my ears while Williams curled up on a couch and talked in his Southern drawl through veils of cigarette smoke. Almost everything was punctuated by a highly infectious chuckle that belied the misery of many of his words ("I have never before been so depressed or found it so hard to work . . ."). He was a small, round, untidy man with a big mustache, the opposite of his spruce, athletic secretary and roommate, Frankie Merlo (the love of Williams' life, who was soon to die of cancer). Merlo let me in and talked politely about Europe until Williams appeared; then he left us alone together, and the amusing Williams' solo began.

James Baldwin's name came up toward the end. Frankie Merlo called from the next room, "Tenn, Anna is on the phone." It was Anna Magnani, the fiery Italian film actress who had said Williams was the only man she'd like to marry. "When will you be ready for dinner?"

"Soon, soon," Williams replied, and went on talking about a book of reminiscences by Eugene O'Neill's second wife. I told him I knew O'Neill's last wife and widow, Carlotta, who lived in a private New York hotel and talked about her dead husband as if he had been her erring child. Williams said he had met Carlotta with Jose Quintero, who had directed the posthumous O'Neill plays at her request. I remembered Mrs. O'Neill's account of the meeting, which she had given me several times, with great relish, over our weekly lunches. She was a rich, rather puritanical woman who obviously greatly disapproved of Tennessee Williams because of his homosexuality. She had told me scathingly that Williams had turned up half-drunk with a boyfriend and he had said to her wasn't it true that Eugene O'Neill had had a deep secret, a side he hadn't revealed to the world? "I knew what he meant," she said, "and I told him, 'My husband wasn't at all like you, Mr. Williams.' " I was about to ask Tennessee Williams for his version, but Merlo looked in at that moment and said apologetically, "Tenn, Anna was on again."

I took the hint and rose to leave. At the door, Williams suddenly said, "Why don't you interview James Baldwin?"

At first I didn't recognize the name and then I remembered a novel I had picked up at a railway bookstall in Europe. It was a paperback with a sensational jacket that stressed the theme of homosexuality. Since it looked like cheap pornography, I nearly didn't buy it, but there was an approving quote from a critic I admired so I chanced it. I was glad I did because it was a moving story about the harm that self-deception can do, a Jamesian theme but written by a Henry James who had lived in the streets. I particularly remembered the vivid description of the seedy gay bars in Paris.

"I liked his *Giovanni's Room*," I told Williams hesitantly.

My hesitation was reasonable then—it seems amusing now. Baldwin wasn't well enough known to interest *The Manchester*

Guardian—it would be hard to sell the editor an interview—
and also I imagined the kind of man he probably was and I had
better things to do during my short visit to New York than
meet him. The chief character of *Giovanni's Room* was a
spoiled white American who helped to destroy his lover so he
wouldn't have to face himself, a classic closet queen. I guessed
the author would be one of those middle-class white Americans
with a private income who would pride himself on being vastly
superior to his character—super-sophisticated, intelligent,
bitchy, gossipy, all the time telling you how gay he was, priding
himself on his honesty—and yet, underneath all the game-
playing and unknown to himself, apparently, really very much
like the character. It was the revenge that literature sometimes
gets on an author. No, to be honest, I wasn't keen to meet Mr.
Baldwin.

"He worked as Gadge Kazan's assistant on *Sweet Bird,*"
Williams said encouragingly. "I'll give you his phone number."

I made a note of it, but it was several days later when I
phoned and then rather reluctantly. I expected an affected
show business voice; the nervous, intense tones came as a surprise. He invited me to come by next day. Did I know where
Horatio Street was? No, I didn't know New York. He gave me
directions. There was a pleasing music in the voice and no
accent I could recognize.

The New York subway system was still a mystery to me so
I went down Ninth Avenue by bus. It was a hot summer day
and, used to a much colder climate, I sweated all the way. By
the time I got off the bus below 14th Street, my shirt was
sticking to me. I imagined Baldwin would be cool and immacu-
late and deodorized and scented and that he would look down
his fine New England nose at my appearance.

I was in a wilderness of gray back streets, the edge of a lonely
warehouse district; I took several wrong turnings before I eventually found Horatio Street. It reminded me of parts of the
East End of London. Baldwin's apartment was upstairs and
was fairly small; with only a few people in it, it seemed over-
crowded. I was surprised to see several blacks there because in

my brief experience of New York, it was very unusual to find interracial groups in white homes. In fact, in Baldwin's apartment there was only one white, a middle-aged man with a high giggle, and so I went over to him to present myself.

"Mr. Baldwin," I began.

He looked vaguely at me, as if he hadn't even heard. I had once gone to interview a movie star and found him very drunk; perhaps now it was my turn with a writer.

"Mr. Baldwin," I repeated.

"Oh, you want Jimmy," a tall young black man said. "He's in the kitchen."

Bottles and glasses were chinking nearby. A small black man appeared with a glass in each hand. His head was formidable, with big, incredibly expressive eyes and a wide mouth that flashed frequent grins. His slight body hardly matched that large head; it was like a frail wire connected to a big bulb that continually lit up: you saw only the light in his face.

"Jimmy, he's looking for *you.*"

Grins between the two blacks as if they were in on some private joke, but it was very good humored and friendly.

"Hi," the small man said, shaking hands.

I realized then the mistake I'd made: *this* was Baldwin; I'd completely misread *Giovanni's Room.* Because there were no black characters in the novel, it never occurred to me that the author might be black. Blacks wrote about blacks—right? And yet Giovanni in a way was playing a black role, the victim of white self-deception. Surely, too, I should have realized the strong, direct style and the attitude toward life could not fit the man I had had in mind. Was I misled by the subject, did it open up my own prejudices?

Baldwin gave me a drink of Scotch and introduced me around. The young black who had taken me to him was Tony Maynard (later to be involved in a murder case that was to drag on for seven years before he proved his innocence); another young black was an artist named Lorenzo Hail. The white man I'd taken for Baldwin was a professor, and everyone seemed to enjoy the fact, including the professor. Baldwin clearly had a gift for making you feel relaxed and welcome; I felt more like a guest at a party than an interviewer.

Baldwin was wearing an open-necked, short-sleeved shirt and dark pants; he seemed to spend no more time on his appearance than I did. Tony Maynard was more elegant with a proud bearing that, with his mane of black hair, reminded me of a young lion; Lorenzo Hail was more casual, more gentle, with a dreamer's eyes. A bust of Baldwin by Lorenzo was on a table; it was a very good likeness of the man and a fine bust in its own right. Lorenzo worked in a local post office, but wanted to give all his time to art. He had the American black artist's dream that Europe might set him free and give him his opportunity. It had worked for Jimmy, why not for him?

I kept reminding myself I was there to interview Baldwin and I tried the occasional interviewer's question and learned he'd been born in Harlem, the eldest of nine children; his father was dead, but his mother still lived in Harlem . . . But it was no good—the questions and answers had to make their way through a lot of laughter and party talk among the others, and finally Baldwin threw up his hands in mock despair. "As you don't know anyone in New York, join us tonight. I've got to go to my publisher's first and then we're going by a friend's house. We could meet there or, as you don't know New York, it might be better to meet Tony in a bar and go with him. We could talk then."

He was friendly and considerate; it was the advantage of meeting someone before he became famous and had less free time. He also had a special feeling for Europe and Europeans. Europe had been a refuge for him, and here was I, a European, seeking the same thing in his country. He would help if he could, if only to repay favors he had received.

So it was all arranged and Baldwin prepared for a trip uptown to his publisher's. He talked about the journey the way Moses must have talked about going up the mountain. His only suit, dark and rather worn, came out of the closet. Clean shirt, tie. Soon he looked businesslike and prepared for battle. Going to meet The Man.

I spent the time from then until I had to meet Tony Maynard catching up with Baldwin's other books in a local library. There weren't many. A first novel, *Go Tell It on the Mountain,* was set in Harlem and I assumed it was largely autobiographical. It was an eloquent tale of Good and Evil in the ghetto. The chief character was a boy preacher whose religious faith takes a battering from reality, "hanging there with darkness all around him." The boy and his family were vividly described; on one level, the novel was a superb portrait of family life. But I was to be haunted for years by a slight love story, just a few pages of the book, involving a young man named Richard who called his girl friend "Little-bit." Richard was wrongly arrested and the police, to justify their mistake, tried to beat a confession out of him. He committed suicide, "his eyes staring upward with no light, dead among the scarlet sheets." As a former police reporter I had seen plenty of police violence, and I knew exactly what Baldwin was getting at. I also knew that Richard and Little-bit must be based on real people; Baldwin had been paying some heavy dues in that novel.

His other book, *Notes of a Native Son,* was a loose collection of essays, partly about America, partly about Europe, but all with the common theme of discovery of what it meant to be black in white society. Coupled with the two novels I had read, it described Baldwin's discovery that he was "different"; at first there was a feeling that this was a misfortune because it meant you had fewer advantages, but slowly the tide of understanding turned and you could see the writer's growing excitement at the realization that this very difference could be turned to advantage—that it could be a source of great riches if you could fully explore the meaning of being black. *Go Tell It on the Mountain* and *Giovanni's Room* began to seem complimentary, the one telling of the black condition, the other explaining how this had come about by the self-deception of the privileged. The two novels were like the two sides of a coin and *Notes of a Native Son* put them together, underlining their meaning. Baldwin, for all his friendliness, obviously had great anger inside him; it might be like keeping the company of a volcano.

We met as arranged; his visit to his publisher's must have been satisfactory because he was in a good mood. At the friend's apartment on 18th Street, a young man asked him to look at his poetry. Baldwin gave the verses long and careful attention; I sensed that he liked the young man rather better than his poetry but he didn't show it, and I was struck again by his kindness. The young poet, like me, was white, and yet Baldwin didn't take his anger and sorrow, so powerfully described in his books, out on us.

I asked him if the character of Richard in *Go Tell It on the Mountain* had been based on a friend of his. He sighed; yes, it had been a friend. I made some reference to the police, about how the uniform corrupted so many. He gave me a quick glance, as if reappraising me. "Ever been on the receiving end?" he asked.

"I was a police reporter for a couple of years."

"Ever been taken on a vacant lot and beaten up?"

No, I hadn't.

He shrugged then, as if I couldn't know what life was like. He made me feel defensive—was the volcano going to erupt? But he suddenly smiled. "Let's not get into that."

I asked him if *Go Tell It on the Mountain* had been based on his own childhood. "Yes," he said, "it comes out of those years I was a preacher—I began when I was fourteen and I stopped when I was seventeen. Very soon afterward I left home. The story came out of that part of my life and I rewrote it God knows how many times. But it also comes out of all the influences on me as a writer—the Bible, the storefront churches, the irony and understatement in Negro speech, all my reading in favorite writers like Dickens, but perhaps above all, my slow realization that Shakespeare, Bach, Rembrandt, Chartres, the Empire State Building did not really contain my history; they were not my heritage. I was an interloper from Africa, but the jungle was not my home; I would therefore have to take over these white centuries and make them mine, make them work for me, a part of me on *my* terms." His eyes were wide now, his right hand gesturing. "I sometimes don't under-

10

stand white people," he said, "but I'm working at it, and I've always understood them a lot more than they've ever understood *me.*" He touched my hand impulsively. "Don't take what I say personally."

"Perhaps I should."

"Perhaps it's for you to decide."

Was there now an undercurrent of hostility? Would I be forced into a symbolic role?

I waited, but Baldwin didn't follow up. The threatened storm had passed. I once more felt European, not white. The professor arrived, even tighter than he'd been before, and the party was on again. While we were drinking, Baldwin said to me suddenly, "Anger is a waste of time, but it's inevitable. It's not open to any arguments whatever."

"In your essay on your father, you say hatred never fails to destroy the person who hates."

"That's right." He seemed pleased that I knew his work so well. Could he guess that I'd only read up on him that afternoon?

"You also say that we not only have to accept the world as it is but must also never stop trying to change it for the better."

"That's about what I believe," he said.

The professor came over to accuse him of being too serious. "You're sitting there pontificating like Henry James, Jimmy."

Baldwin flashed me his wide-open grin; he gave the impression of a great capacity for enjoying himself, the deceptive other side of the volcano.

"Let's rejoin the party."

I went to Detroit to spend a few days with an old friend and his wife. Baldwin had told me he and Tony were planning to spend a week in the Michigan woods so we arranged that they would spend a night at my friend's. He was an easygoing ex-reporter and I assumed my invitation would be welcomed by him. He had never heard of Baldwin so I gave him a copy of *Giovanni's Room.* Much to my surprise, it seemed to make him uneasy. He asked me cautiously whether it was autobiographical; I was impressed by the novel's power to shock. He began to make me feel sorry I'd invited Baldwin—what was I letting him in for? But the day Baldwin was supposed to arrive came and went without his showing up. I was rather relieved. My relations with the old friend were never the same again.

When I returned to New York, I phoned Baldwin, concerned that something might have happened to him. He was there. No, nothing had happened; he'd just had to stay in the city for business. It had clearly never occurred to him to let me know he wasn't coming.

I went around some of the Village bars with him that night —all kinds of drinking places, from workingmen's Irish bars to sleek show business hangouts. I remember one basement bar in particular, mainly gay. The young barman received Baldwin as if he were a prince and asked him to autograph a copy of *Giovanni's Room.* Several people in the bar stopped talking to watch Baldwin; here he was already famous. Baldwin took advantage of his status to ask the barman to cash a check for him; it was a sign of power that pleased him, as if it was a herald of fame on the horizon. Not long now, the signs seemed to say; hang in there, Jimmy.

He told me that *Giovanni's Room* might possibly become a play and a movie. "Times are slowly changing," he said with a satisfied expression. "In this bar, a lot of people identify with *Giovanni;* they feel as oppressed as Negroes. But a break-through is coming, a willingness to listen. Great changes are on the way. It's hard to remember how difficult it was to get *Giovanni* accepted here. They told me to burn it!" His voice rose indignantly, dramatically. "They said it would ruin me if I tried to get it published. I had turndowns because they treated it like pornography. But I wouldn't accept such treat-ment. I took it over to England and my publisher there said if his lawyers passed it, he'd love to publish it. And there were no problems. None at all. The book got good reviews. And once the English accepted it so well, the cowards here took it. Never talk to me about the *courage* of American publishers. You're stupid if you let their rejections worry you—and I say that as one who was stupid. Always make up your own mind. You just can't afford to let people give you your evaluation of yourself. Certainly not if you're a Negro. If I've learned one thing from life, that's it. . . ."

When he was at his most intense, the boy preacher's mannerisms appeared; he used his face and his hands like an actor. I was always surprised when I read descriptions of him as an ugly man. His face was so lively, his eyes and his mouth so expressive that the impression he always left was incredibly vivid. His appearance wasn't ugly but eccentric, so much more interesting than a conventionally handsome person. But I felt sometimes that Baldwin would have given all his talents for self-expression to have the handsome, humdrum good looks of the average beach boy. Big muscles, a face—as Aldous Huxley put it—like a battering ram. That might have been a dream in a weak moment.

But never, I'm sure, was his dream of being white. The anger was too deep and genuine. I believed him when he told me that night, "I do *not* hate white people. I haven't got enough emotional energy. There are some people I hate, some are white, some are black." Occasionally, to back the feeling of his words, he liked to touch the person he was speaking to, a sort of laying on of hands to convey emotion physically. He gripped my hand then as he said, "The only time you'll hear nonviolence admired is when black men preach and practice it. Whites admire violence in themselves." He stared at me as if waiting for my disagreement. "Remember, to hate, to be violent, is demeaning. It means you're afraid of the other side of the coin—to love and be loved."

We stood over drinks, talking for a long time; Baldwin remembered coming to the Village before he had fled to France.

"I came here in my late teens; the Village was terrifying at first. I was a kid, and I didn't know nothin' from nothin'; white women and white men—who looked like Truman or Eisenhower—took advantage of me in grotesque ways. For such people, homosexuality is just the other side of heterosexuality and nobody makes any connections. It's not love or sex; it's too clinical. If you're a black kid, you're a victim for all these sad males and their fantasies. It's not fear of sex between men; it's fear of people touching each other. White people have to learn how to accept and love themselves and each other; when they've done that, the Negro Problem will no longer exist, because it won't be needed any longer. But I mustn't get on my soapbox."

He began to reminisce about his boyhood. He was nick-named "Froggy" or "Popeyes" at school, and even today, he said, it was hard not to get mad if anyone made a crack about his eyes. "I was unbelievably shy. I helped to bring up my brothers and sisters, sitting at the table with a baby in one arm and a book in the other. The first book I read through was *Uncle Tom's Cabin.* I read it so many times I nearly wore it out. Slowly I discovered that according to society, I was a *nigger.* It was hard to accept and I decided to refuse! I decided that whatever I did wouldn't be on society's terms but on my own. I would do anything to survive; they would hear from me. I was out there shining shoes, being a porter, handyman, eleva-tor operator, and I discovered how monstrous people can be, especially when I worked among a lot of white Southerners in New Jersey. They thought I was very cocky and gave me hell. I felt a rage like fever, and I learned that you have to find a way of living with it or you just have to surrender to it. I wasn't going to surrender to anything or anybody."

Baldwin told me about those times as though he were reliv-ing the experiences, his eyes wide and far away, his voice hushed and dramatic. His father died, leaving his mother with eight small children. He decided he had to achieve something before she died or all the children were jailed or became junkies or whores. "I discovered writing. It was an act of love, a way perhaps to save me and my family. I had to make a great gamble, but I really had so little to lose it wasn't so difficult. I had no real formal education. How dare I be a writer! But I had patience and great determination. Richard Wright en-couraged me, but when my first novel was rejected by publish-ers, it took me a long time to get up again. A friend jumped

14

off the George Washington Bridge in despair and I knew I had to get away—I've always known when to leave the party. I decided I had to go for broke. I bought a one-way plane ticket to France, not knowing whether I was black or white, male or female, rich or poor, talented or a fraud, strong or merely obstinate. I was a mess and I knew I had to get away to put myself together and survive. I was scared shitless, but I've always been scared, and if you're scared enough, there's nothing left to be scared of. That's the point I'd reached when I left this country."

I walked him back to his apartment through the dark side streets. We were both pretty high and I found myself arguing with him—I think it was about Faulkner—and even having the last word. He didn't get annoyed when I shouted him down, but listened politely. It was one of the nice things about meeting someone before they became famous: they had time to listen to you.

2

When I first met Norman Mailer early in 1961, he was already famous and so I would never know him as well as I came to know Baldwin.

Mailer's long novel about World War II, *The Naked and the Dead,* had established him overnight as a literary celebrity. But he hadn't tried to cling to success by repeating himself. His second novel, *Barbary Shore,* couldn't have been more different. It was a short, bleak political novel that reflected his experiences with existentialism in Paris after the war. Many of the people who had praised *The Naked and the Dead* hated *Barbary Shore,* and his overnight success was threatened. His third novel, *The Deer Park,* an explicitly political and sexual picture of Hollywood during the witch-hunts, was rejected by six publishers before it was accepted by the seventh. Mailer's courage and obstinacy reminded me of Baldwin's refusal to accept the rejection of *Giovanni's Room;* turning initial defeats into eventual triumphs, they had overcome some of the prejudices of their time against sexual honesty. Other writers would be freer in future because of their efforts.

Because Mailer was famous, I was better prepared for meeting him. I had read his three novels and some of his essays—and much of the publicity about his personal activities. He was such a clever self-promoter that most of his life seemed to get into the public domain eventually. He had acquired a reputation as an *enfant terrible,* mixing with the postwar hipster-drug scene and getting involved in some well-publicized brawls.

Seeing photographs of him and following the gossip columns, I knew what to expect. He was obviously an Irish-American, the kind that practically owned the New York City police force. A quarter Irish myself (or more if I accepted an old boyhood swap with my brother), I fancied myself an expert on them. Mailer's combination of boyish, self-deprecating humor and a wary look around the eyes reminded me of some of my Irish relatives and friends. They'd be preaching Catholicism to you one minute and trying to pick a fight with you the next; when they had you lulled into thinking what charming, generous, modest, loving people they were, that was the time to be most on your guard, or you'd fall for a sucker punch.

Mailer's blend of charm and aggression, I convinced myself, was pure Irish. He had that outsider's feeling of the Irish that was best summed up by Joseph Kennedy, the patriarch of the Kennedy family: "I was born in the United States and so was my father before me but my children are still called Irish. What the hell do we have to do to become Americans?" If you have this feeling, you try to ingratiate, to plot, to buy your way in, but coupled with this ambition is a feeling of aggression, even hatred, at not being accepted for yourself. No wonder Irishman Mailer felt such sympathy for fellow Irishman John Kennedy in the White House. He even claimed some credit for his election because Kennedy had squeezed in by so few votes that Mailer's approval might just have swung enough hipster votes his way. Irishmen clearly had to stick together; in spite of his hipster experiments, Mailer even showed a decent respect for Irish cops—or was that just an ingratiating Irishman's respect for anybody with power?

I first met him in the flesh at London Airport when he was arriving to promote a new collection of his essays—entitled with charming frankness and devious cunning, *Advertisements for Myself.* He had recently been involved in a much-publicized early-morning drama after a party he and his wife had given. The guests had departed and some time later he had stabbed

17

his wife with a penknife. With this on their minds, the assembled greeters at the airport were clearly expecting a combination of Rimbaud and De Quincey to come shambling out of the customs shed.

He appeared with the same sheepish grin that Brendan Behan, the Dublin writer, showed when reporters waited for him to appear noisily drunk. But Behan, a real Irishman, had lacked the driving ambition that America seemed to give the clan, an ambition Mailer typified. Mailer had the look of a little boy who knows he's been bad and is unsure of how he will be received. It was still so soon after the stabbing incident that Mailer didn't yet know how it would affect his public standing. Maybe he'd finally gone too far. Although his wife hadn't pressed charges, he'd shown great concern when the New York police had taken him in that he might be certified as mentally unbalanced—people would have had an excuse then for not taking his future work seriously. A friend of Mailer's had advised me not to mention the stabbing incident unless he brought it up first, and he made only a veiled reference to it when he told reporters that he had given up his idea of running for mayor of New York as an existentialist candidate "because I think I have now thoroughly disqualified myself." His political ambitions seemed to fit in, too, with my picture of him as the ambitious Irishman; they always looked for power through local politics.

How wrong I was. As wrong as I was about Baldwin being an effete New Englander. Mailer told me that day his favorite quotation was from André Gide: "Please do not understand me too quickly." In my dash to understand him, I had fallen for too easy an explanation. When in conversation with him I probed sympathetically for his Irish roots, expecting a little revealing pain, the truth soon fell out. He was Jewish, not Irish! It surprised me as much as the discovery that Baldwin was black.

I should have been warned by Mailer's novel, *The Deer Park,* in which the hero, Sergius O'Shaugnessy, discovers he's "a false Irishman." Instead I'd assumed that giving a hero the impossible name of Sergius O'Shaugnessy was just another Irishman's tribute to the old country and another blow for independence from his aggressive, independent side. Now, instead of the Irish rebel, Mailer was transformed before my eyes into a Jewish rebel—a rebel from his upbringing in Brooklyn as a nice Jewish boy with the softness of someone early accustomed to mother love.

Jews had a deeper, more permanent sense of being outsiders than the Irish; sometimes this feeling of not being accepted drove them to such extremes as changing their names and pretending they weren't Jewish. Was any of this at the back of Mailer's hearty Irish personality or was it merely a personal joke, like his terrible imitation of English accents? Would his feeling of exclusion as a Jew help him to understand the black situation? Probably not, for Jews and blacks rarely sympathized with each other. Jews, frantically finding job security through techniques of survival evolved over hundreds of years, seemed unable to grasp why blacks couldn't do the same. Blacks on their side often couldn't understand why Jews were discriminated against and suspected gross exaggeration. They looked white, didn't they? It was a difference of degree, if anything, not of kind. Would such feelings be at the back of Baldwin's and Mailer's minds when they looked at each other?

Mailer set out to charm that day, like a dethroned champion who knows how much work he has to do to win back his crown. He admitted frankly with a boyish grin that perhaps he should hire a public relations man to grease his career. "I started as a generous but very spoiled boy and now I seem to have grown into a slightly punch-drunk club fighter." He hunched his heavy shoulders as if he was going to throw a punch. It was very likeable, like a politician admitting he's trying to con you instead of giving you a righteous message. He interrupted himself to worry about his publisher's secretary, who had worked late to rent him a car. Secretaries are usually background automatons to visiting celebrities, so this was a big mark in favor of his humanity. He seemed even more likeable. "I don't care to approach the public like a lover," he said, but *that* was hard to believe.

The first hurdle successfully cleared—his reception good so far, with no put-down questions about wives or stabbing—he became more serious: the writer at work. Novelists must not write about what had already been dealt with; they must find "new areas of experience," he said. Lately he seemed to have regarded all ordinary ways of life as exhausted subjects and he went to extremes to find virgin fields—"areas of experience that other men are afraid of."

The war was over but the financial success of *The Naked and the Dead* gave him the means to find peacetime substitutes. His first novel had been a picture of the whole of society through the army, of how individuals survive in a conformist structure. His work since seemed like an attempt to define what being an individual meant, the price you had to pay. Much of American society was so conformist it gave him a "shut-out" feeling, he said.

As an example of what he meant, he told me about a recent party given by some small-businessmen and professional types. In a tone of wonderment, he described how they had played party games—charades, Ping-Pong—that contained "not a hint of sex," which would have been impossible at a hipster party, the kind Mailer was more used to. "I didn't know whether it was just complacent, blind, unhealthy, or whether it was really fresh and good and healthy," he said. It was a part of society he had been shut out of for years—or had shut himself out of—probably since his Harvard days.

Ah, yes, he had gone to Harvard. He said gruffly he'd gone there to study aeronautical engineering at the same time he was discovering modern American literature; he might have gone to MIT, he added mischievously, but he wanted to be with a good football team. It was obviously not a subject that interested him; his Harvard education seemed to embarrass him that day; he was much keener to talk about World War II or hipsters. And he seemed obsessed by the idea that "sex is the only new frontier left for a writer to explore." To justify this belief, he often seemed to simplify life and people's reaction to it.

There was a revealing example in a disagreement with William Faulkner (which he reported in *Advertisements for Myself*). Young writers like to take on old ones in the hope of making a reputation, just as young gunslingers used to challenge the old fastest-on-the-draw killers in the West; Mailer had taken on Faulkner just as Baldwin had finally challenged his old patron, Richard Wright. Mailer had reduced the problem of segregation in the deep South to sexual fear. "Everybody who knows the South knows that the white man fears the sexual potency of the Negro." When Mailer sent him a copy of this statement, Faulkner, who had lived most of his life in Mississippi, commented: "I have heard this idea expressed several times during the last twenty years, though not before by a man. The others were ladies, Northern or Middle Western ladies, usually around forty or forty-five years of age. I don't know what a psychiatrist would find in this." Mailer replied, "Like many novelists who have created an extraordinary body of work, Faulkner is a timid man who has led a sheltered life. So I would not be surprised if he has had his best and most intense conversations with sensitive, middle-aged ladies." And so on, ending with an expression of mock surprise that Faulkner "should think a psychiatrist could ever understand a writer."

Since Faulkner had described sexual fears in novels and short stories, I assumed that he was objecting to Mailer's over-simplification, the feeling that he was merely using the racial situation to make a point. Mailer came out of the encounter seeming like the young challenger who had taken on the fastest-on-the-draw before he was quite ready. I didn't, however, dare say so that day. I didn't want to spoil the atmosphere of friendliness Mailer was beginning to bask in, ready now for his drive in to London and whatever reception awaited him there.

I arranged to see him next day at his publisher's office. Twenty-four hours made a lot of difference. He sat in the office so confident of his reception that he could joke about his publisher's giving me a free copy of his latest book, insisting

21

that everyone should pay for it. He was in a mood to talk— as a writer. Attempts to get him to talk as a Jewish boy from Brooklyn or as a would-be politician got nowhere.

"The best thing to be said for writing is that a lazy man can sometimes make a living at it," he said cheerfully. "I'm not only lazy, I'm a chameleon. Three whiffs of English air and here I'm talking like an Englishman." I didn't like to tell him how poor his imitation English accent was so I just smiled; some day I'd get back at him with a Brooklyn accent. I began to question him about his roots. "I was born in New Jersey. My father was a South African who came to the United States in 1920, after First World War service, via England. I took writing courses each year at Harvard. People say they teach you what not to do, but I think their help is more subtle. You get a sense of audience. You learn very early what reactions are going to be and how much you might be willing to tailor something for a market or whether you must remain independent. You learn about your own character as a writer. To be independent to me means something pretty good."

He sat back, feeling satisfied. I tried to shake him out of his attitude by a question about his first attempts at novel writing.

"I wrote a novel in college," he said, "and another after I got out. Neither was published. Perhaps it was fortunate. The first novel was very bad—autobiographical stuff you write when you are eighteen or nineteen. The second was about a mental hospital, based on experience when I worked in one briefly during a vacation between junior and senior year. It was a vicious, murky, symbolical novel, a terribly cumbersome thing. In the army I served in the Philippines—Leyte, Luzon —as a rifleman. After the war I became a T4, a sergeant techni-cian fourth grade. I was a cook. That's right, I wrote a short story about it. I didn't do any writing in the army but I used to write letters home to my first wife. There was a big pile when I got out and some served as notes when I came to write *The Naked and the Dead.*"

He began to talk about that big, enormously successful first novel almost as if it had been written by someone else. "I had

22

been thinking about it all during the war. It was the easiest book I ever had to write—the easiest of the published books. Its success was like having a great love affair when you are fourteen. I started writing another novel but after about fifty pages I had to stop. I tried to start a third novel but it didn't go at all. Then I went back to the second one, which eventually became *Barbary Shore.* It wasn't only success that was worrying me. It was more a matter of having used up one kind of material completely. I wanted to write something entirely different, in a different key. I had been influenced by one sort of writer; Thomas Wolfe and Tolstoy were the two I thought about most. I kept *Anna Karenina* on my desk while I was writing *The Naked and the Dead.* Then I went to Paris and the influences changed. I was very struck by Christopher Isherwood. I read *Goodbye to Berlin* and loved it. Faulkner and Hemingway came later as influences—Faulkner for *Barbary Shore* and Hemingway for *The Deer Park."*

It flowed out of him now; I hardly needed to prompt him with a question. He might have been an elder statesman talking about his rise to the top.

"In *The Deer Park* I was trying to find a style for the story and it was very elusive. I went through four drafts. The first draft was Proustian—not first-rate Proust of course. The second draft was somewhere between the English novel of manners and Fitzgerald; I'm not saying as good but in that direction. The third draft was more Hemingway. Then I found my own style, which was nothing like these. Part of finding your style is losing your excessive admiration for the styles of other writers.

"Then after *The Deer Park* there was a complete change again. In *Advertisements* there's the occasional piece with a little more specific density to it; it's a bit more intense and less discursive."

I tried to get him talking about the relationship between his experience and what he wrote about.

"It depends on the kind of writer you are," he said. "I don't think of myself simply as a realist, though it's a tradition which is pleasant and comfortable for me. But there are very elusive things one wants to say. You can't get at them just by using accurate dialogue and realistic characters. Since *The Naked and the Dead,* my experience has altered very profoundly—it's been more indiscriminate and less traditional. It's been existentialist. I lost the categories into which I could fit experience. I lost that comfortable sense of proportion which made it so easy to write *The Naked and the Dead,* which came out of all the books I loved in college. I felt I needed a new style. In some ways terribly difficult to describe, the style often becomes the vision. I mean, one can capture or fail to capture difficult experience. It can often be transmuted by mood, and style is the ground of all mood—to use Heidegger's word.

"The thing that always fascinated me about style is the way in which it literally repels certain kinds of experience. The more powerful style becomes, the more complex the subjects you can write about with equal authority. The style begins to select the material. I think that's happened with my last few books. If a person keeps a certain style, it determines the experience that comes to him. But my style is constantly changing by twists and starts. So's my experience. Is it a conscious search for experience? Oh, don't get misled by the headlines of my life. Very often a reputation develops from very little. It doesn't take much to make a legend. Your experience more or less selects itself.

"The American social structure, you see, is unbelievably complicated. It's amazing how many places one is not invited to. Vast areas of experience, of society, one can't get near. Vast numbers of people you just don't get a chance to meet. And often you are excluded effectively even if you aren't officially —because the moment you get too far from the sort of thing you have been doing the more unnaturally people react to you. I have only to write about sex and people take me for a sex maniac. Obviously there's no point in having experience just for the sake of having experience. The experience you write about is the experience that gets way into you."

He was enjoying himself—not as a born preacher like Baldwin, religion and singing the blues all blended together—but more as a pundit, those Harvard years showing in spite of being suppressed.

"If you are obliged in your experience to go in deeply, you're sometimes considered a gargoyle. But then occasionally even that kind of experience has a way of returning to the surface, and you're left with mere satire instead of psychic penetration. The price of being independent is to be shut out of the group. And perhaps then you develop a tendency to write about people even more shut out than yourself. Once you develop a reputation as a gargoyle, the only place you find a community of sympathy is with other gargoyles."

Was the Jewish boy beginning to show in that remark about being shut out of the group? What an effort it must take for a Jew—and even more a black—to give up the comfort of the group's protection against oppression! In his early essays that searched for the meaning of being black in America, Baldwin had made many enemies in Harlem; the black establishment wanted no part of someone with such outlaw views, someone they couldn't use. Mailer in a way had gone even further by not even identifying himself in any meaningful way as Jewish, unlike other contemporary writers such as Arthur Miller, Saul Bellow, Bernard Malamud. There was literary market value in claiming to be Jewish because Jews bought and even read books; but it obviously went against the grain with Mailer to put his Jewishness mid-stage, it offended some outlaw image he had of himself; and probably he would be in as bad with the Jewish establishment as Baldwin was with the black equivalent uptown. Only a general success, not dependent on groups or establishments, would protect them from the eventual put-down that awaited everyone in American life without group protection who ventured out there alone.

Yet why was it that one was so much more conscious of these nonconformist nightmares in Mailer's presence than in Baldwin's? A black born in Harlem *lived* a nightmare of insecurity from his childhood on. A Jewish boy from Brooklyn who could make it to Harvard had been born into comparative safety; he could afford to face reality. But perhaps, having known security, and the life of the privileged—though that was a hard fact for a Jew to accept after centuries of persecution—he had been subtly weakened. He knew what he was missing, and when times were hard out there among the outlaws who lead individual, independent existences, there must be a tremendous urge, an all-but-irresistible temptation to go back home, back to that comfortable womb. Was this what had worried Mailer—that the scandal over the stabbing might mean he could *never* go back?

I remembered discussing with Robert Frost his lines "I never dared be radical when young/ For fear it would make me conservative when old," and Frost told me he had had in mind middle-class boys who gave up the comfort they were born into to save society and how, in his experience, when they began to age and slow down, they always went back to the life they had rejected. "It takes a good man to remain alone," he said. "And you usually have to die young." Were these lines haunting Mailer at this crossroads in his life?

And did they also explain why Baldwin's favorite expression was to "go for broke"? Baldwin had never had to make the choice of being radical; his color automatically made him a radical in American society. To free himself, he didn't need to reject the safe home he was afraid of conforming to, but the *outsiders* whom he saw as responsible for the fact that his home *wasn't* safe, secure, the haven a child deserved. His temptation would be the reverse of Mailer's—not to go back but to be forever haunted by the fear of going back to the point he had started from. The Jewish boy would always be wooing Mailer the outlaw, whereas the Harlem boy would be forever frightening Baldwin—however far away he got on other continents, however much money he had in the bank.

Mailer turned everything back to his role as the extremist of experience, imprisoning me in the part of straight-man interviewer. On the surface, people might have said he and I had more in common than Baldwin and I; blacks certainly would have supposed our white skins would automatically draw us

26

together. But I meant no more personally to Mailer than I had to politicians when I interviewed them; I was merely the means for them to put over what they wanted. Baldwin, I suppose, had the choice of doing that, but my whiteness was a challenge to him, whereas it wasn't to Mailer. Baldwin could reject me, dehumanize me for that reason as many blacks did, or he could accept its challenge and look for the individual beneath it. Baldwin didn't allow himself a choice at that time. Perhaps, too, it had something to do with the price of fame. Mailer had had not only years of contending with fame, with American Success, but also with struggling to overcome failure afterward and regain the top before he fell back into the arms of the Jewish boy. That stabbing incident seemed more and more like a colossal risk, the gambler's final throw with his life. Was that the price not of fame but of truly meaningful experience? Was Mailer willing to "go for broke"?

"Many people have told me," he was saying easily, smoothly, filling his role now, "the English have a greater love for authentic characters. My ideas haven't really changed since *Advertisements.* I suspect they have become slightly more civilized, more palatable, but that's not necessarily an improvement. Extreme experience isn't necessarily perverted from being a universal theme. If I ever finished the large novel I'm on now, I'll have written about extreme experience as if it's nonextreme. One can break through the psychic sound barrier and then extreme experience becomes quite logical. Dostoevsky was able to write about Raskolnikov and make him a perfectly comprehensible character to everybody. Today the average American writer would make Raskolnikov a gargoyle or a monster."

I tried to edge Mailer back from his outlaw role by asking him about his beliefs, thinking perhaps he might deal with religion and his early training as a Jew. But it was like asking Jean Genêt to play a policeman; he simply used the question the way he wanted to.

"My beliefs? Things look much more complicated now than they used to. Life seems insuperably complicated. But I think we're in need of a real vigorous underground to keep Western culture alive. For me, the real danger is not that the Russians will take over and put an end to our civilization; it is that the West will lose its historic marrow through compromises and deliberate failure to think things through. Let's go back to some of the old answers, for one of the bad things we must realize is that if the Russians came, the very people who are screaming against them now would be the ones who would work with them."

It was a good exit line; end of interview. He hunched his shoulders again and gave me that blend of boyish grin and wary assessment of how I was taking it. He reminded me then of a smaller Hemingway—perhaps it was the boxer's stance and the talk about the "large novel." Hemingway was always talking about his Big Novel as if trying to build up reader suspense, one of Hemingway's tricks of self-promotion that Mailer himself called Notes from Papa on How the Working Novelist Can Get Ahead. Other writers, like Capote and James Jones, had also learned the tricks.

Baldwin, of course, wouldn't identify with Hemingway, who seemed to have had it easy. Baldwin instead would study how Richard Wright had tried to make it. Just as Mailer had taken on the giants on his—white—side, Faulkner and Hemingway (". . . the best tactic to hide the lockjaw of his shrinking genius was to become the personality of our time . . ."), so Baldwin had first allowed Richard Wright to be his guide and then, feeling the strength of his own talent, had begun to reject him when he went to France ("I was always exasperated by his notions of society, politics and history, for they seemed to me utterly fanciful . . .").

Mailer had a good press in London; it carried back to New York. The work of undoing the harm of the stabbing scandal had begun. I wondered what Mailer had decided—that he had gone too far and must retrench and know his limits, or whether this marked the point of no return and he would go on from there. I sensed in what he had said, but above all in his manner-isms, his tough-guy talk about not wanting to be loved all the

28

while his manner indicated the opposite, that he still itched to play a role of action—another Hemingway or, better still, an André Malraux. If so, he would have to get back to the point where he might consider running for political office, for that was the only route to power in America unless he wanted to be gunned down by the police or pursued by the FBI; the Red scare of the forties and fifties had drawn the line for radical behavior. What was it Mailer had said on his arrival—that he had "thoroughly disqualified" himself from running for mayor of New York? Was enormous ambition still at the back of that complex, subtle mind?

If so, how long would it take him to become "qualified" again, without turning his back on the person he had become and embracing the nice Jewish boy again? Could he be both extremist and politician? These were rocky, changing times in which a comparatively young Catholic had made it to the White House. Admittedly the Kennedy money had given the president a compensating respectability, but even so, he'd only just made it. Mailer had more than two strikes against him: he was a writer-extremist and he was a Jew—and he had no compensating millions. His chances of playing the power game didn't seem worth giving up much that meant anything to him, but perhaps he saw it differently as he realized that the scandal in New York had not flattened him. It may even have begun to seem a clever gambit to get away and earn forgiveness in England, where decorum and respectability were so prized—at least in the circles visiting Americans usually encountered. In his clever way, Mailer had also appreciated that tolerance of nonconformity was growing greater; he had made a shrewd move, it seemed to me then, but I couldn't guess what direction it was going to take him in.

3

While I was away from New York, I received a form from the
Guggenheim Foundation, asking questions about Lorenzo Hail.
He had applied for a grant and had put my name down as one
of his references; Baldwin was another. Knowing a little about
the politics of grant giving, I didn't think Lorenzo had much
of a chance if the best-known people he could come up with
were Baldwin and me.

Baldwin, I sensed, had an ambition as large as Mailer's, and
his blackness would be an added incentive to outdo the white
boys in his case—other blacks might take it as a reason for a
bitter withdrawal from battle, but not Baldwin; the early shy-
ness of "Popeyes," rocking the babies and hiding in books, had
developed into a scrappy insistence on being given his due;
after all, I could hear him saying in that high-strung voice, he'd
paid for it—paid more than most people. He'd been awarded
grants for his writing on the say-so of white people; how angry
he would be if his name wasn't enough to win one for Lorenzo!

I met him again in New York after I'd been on a reporting
trip down South and I asked for news of Lorenzo Hail. He
hadn't got the grant but he'd set off for France and Italy,
anyway, to study the great sculptors on their own grounds.
"I'm proud of him," Baldwin said. It was the kind of decision
he'd made himself years ago. But he was also clearly annoyed,
as I had anticipated; Guggenheims went to many far less tal-

ented people, he said, but then of course they were white, with the right recommenders. I said jokingly that even my whiteness hadn't made me right; maybe, I suggested, I should have asked Norman Mailer when I met him to speak up for Lorenzo—maybe Mailer could have swung it, at least before the stabbing incident.

Baldwin tensed in a strange way and smiled warily. "You know Norman?" he asked carefully, watching me with less open friendliness, as if he saw me professionally for the first time, whereas of course with Mailer it had been the opposite —he never saw me personally.

I briefly described my meeting and my reaction. Baldwin relaxed, himself again, his suspicion laid to rest. Had paranoia briefly showed—the paranoia of blacks who felt that however friendly you were with whites, they could betray you to other whites? Or was he thinking about his own relations with Mailer?

"Norman and I used to be friends," he said sadly. "I met him in Paris at the home of Jean Malaquais; Norman called him his mentor at that time. I liked him. Our styles were very different —I was a black boy from Harlem and Norman's a middle-class Jew—but we had a lot in common, even a bad habit of suspecting that others are trying to put us down and therefore striking first at *them.*"

Baldwin laughed. "The time came, of course, when we faced each other the same way—suspiciously—and struck. We've never really been friends since." He was drinking Scotch and took a long pull. "The friendship between a black boy and a white boy is a very complex matter, indeed, and Norman and I didn't survive it. You know, there's this difference always to contend with: the white always thinks he has something to lose, even if it's only his innocence. Whereas I've always felt I had nothing—nothing!—to lose. For a long time, I could never take the troubles of white people seriously. They seemed to be born so lucky. No wonder they were all nostalgic for some security they had known in their childhoods; it was a dream they couldn't altogether give up and frequently they gave up their lives for it. I'm sure a part of Norman is still back in that way of life that sent him to Harvard—and being Norman he deeply resents feeling that way.

"What I respected about him at that first meeting was that he didn't pull rank on me. He was famous and I wasn't, he had money and I hadn't, he was white with all its advantages. But then I didn't pull rank on him either, though being black I knew far more about that kind of extreme outlaw experience he was pursuing than he would ever know. We were trapped in our roles—the roles we had created to help us survive and express the parts of ourselves we wanted to make public. It's a dangerous business; the world lets you create your role and then makes you a prisoner in it—"

"I watched Marilyn Monroe make her last movie," I said. "She was struggling to break out of her role."

"She left it too late," Baldwin said. "She was a born outlaw but she had a white nostalgia for that security she had never known in childhood. Arthur Miller, a middle-class Jewish boy from Brooklyn like Norman, was her answer, and Miller traded nostalgia for nostalgia. His picture of her in *The Misfits* was unreal; it had something in common with Norman's carrying on in *The White Negro.*"

"Mailer impressed me," I said, "by grappling with the theme of individuality in a way contemporary white writers seldom do, but he was really writing from a Jewish point of view, it seemed to me, and not admitting it."

"I thought he maligned the people he was writing about in *The White Negro,*" Baldwin said. "I understand his point, I understand why he had to write it, but it is too late to make those kinds of discoveries. This is not the time of the white man any more; he is fast becoming irrelevant because he's had his chance and blown it and history doesn't give you a second chance. You can't jump back on the bandwagon by claiming to be"—Baldwin's voice rose sarcastically—"A White Negro! The white world created the dead conditions that Negroes have had to cope with for centuries, and now the whites find they are getting caught, too, and are having to cope in ways they weren't prepared for. But why didn't they understand that when the Negroes were out there alone?

"Why didn't Norman write about the black Negro? Because he didn't know enough about it. Okay, I accept that, but also because it didn't touch his own life. Norman is competitive as well as ambitious, even more so than I am, and he can't compete in an essentially black scene without being black. That's what white liberals trying to take over the civil rights movement don't understand. They're in a minor, secondary position, baby, simply because they're white. And Norman doesn't want to play some minor role, any more than I do, so he tries to move the white experience back to the center of the stage . . . but it's too late for that. Remember, a man will face in your life only what he will face in his own. It is no use whites trying to be imitation Negroes; let them face their own thing."

"You mean Mailer should write about being a white Jew?"

"That's one way of putting it." He fixed another drink. "But Norman was trying to break the barrier. How many do that? I had some good evenings with Norman, drinking and arguing. He argued to win as if it was a game. I never liked games. It was a hard time in my life—a love affair was on the rocks, my career as a writer wasn't going right, I was dissatisfied. *Giovanni's Room* was being published and I was scared of how it would be received. God knows I'd had enough warnings. Norman was good enough to speak well of it when it came out—his trouble with *The Deer Park* had created a kind of bond. He invited me to Connecticut for a weekend but I couldn't make it; I wasn't in the mood to spend a weekend with people arguing to win. I liked Norman but I didn't care for some of the people he had around him. Your entourage may suit your own needs and fears, but they can just be a strain for other people.

"I heard about Norman's being involved in a couple of fights in the Village. I couldn't imagine anyone disliking Norman to that extent, though of course I'd run into people in Village bars who hated themselves so much they wanted to take it out on *me*. But Mailer wasn't me. He was The White Negro. I think my objection to *The White Negro* is that it seems to me such

33

an old-white view of blacks. It was written in a prose I found impenetrable and also seemed to be borrowing fashionable Beat attitudes from writers who were much inferior to Norman, like Kerouac. Was this the way he really saw *me?* I couldn't believe it. No wonder we couldn't work it out as friends. What I couldn't understand was why Norman was slumming. Was he so embarrassed that he had been born lucky? He is a first-rate talent who should deal with what he is and not what he would like to be. Why borrow from Negroes? Deal with your *own* problems, your own sense of panic!"

"You didn't see Mailer again?" I was trying to get us off *The White Negro;* it irritated Baldwin too much.

"I saw him at a party, but he seemed so belligerent—pontificating and trying to command the center of attention. We both said we were pleased to see each other and I think we were, but when I asked him to call me, we went through the usual stupid competitive exchange people mock. You call me; no, you call me . . . as if it mattered.

"Then Norman published his feelings about me and other American writers in *Advertisements for Myself.* I was in Paris when it came out and Bill Styron, Jim Jones, and I sat in Jim's living room reading aloud Norman's judgment of our personalities and work. His condescension enraged me. I wondered what had happened to him; he was coming on like God, the maker and breaker of reputations, of lives. I met him later at the Actors Studio where an adaptation of *The Deer Park* was being done. I talked to him about what he'd written, but I was cool about it. He expressed some regrets but said he thought I 'had it coming.' His boxer mannerisms were even more pronounced. And for the first time I began to take his political ambitions seriously. He wanted not only to study power, like all first-rate writers, he wanted to wield it. To me it was copping out. Writers deal in the imagination and sometimes it escapes from their work into their lives and they live a real fantasy. Or sometimes a writer plays a role that becomes stifling to him, a virtual prison for his personality, and he has to end it, bring it crashing down—"

"You think that's what happened at that party when he stabbed his wife?"

"God knows. Maybe Norman began to realize where his political ambitions were taking him, the company he'd have to keep, and he struck out blindly. I respect his mastering the fear of experience—it's a general American fear and few American writers overcome it. But such willingness to experience conflicts with any political ambitions and maybe Norman is beginning to realize that. It might be salutary for New York to have such a man running for office, but for Norman it would be escaping the responsibilities of being a writer by trying to become something else—a nothing probably. If Norman's lucky, the stabbing incident will have taken any choice away from him. He'll be stuck with just being a writer."

I wondered if my discovery of Mailer's Jewishness was leading me to exaggerate its importance. I probably did in the case of *The White Negro.* He had made much of the psychic havoc of the concentration camps. I wondered if one didn't have to be Jewish to feel deeply such havoc, just as one had to be black to feel the havoc of segregation and the years of lynching. My own psychic havoc of World War II came from the bombings; my childhood had been spent partly in air-raid shelters—the Germans were trying to kill *me!* I never met an American who felt the same way about the war, simply because America hadn't been bombed; there was no direct experience to draw upon.

It was no accident that Mailer made much of something that Baldwin, for example, couldn't feel with the same intensity. He was reflecting where he'd come from; the Brooklyn Jewish boy was speaking through the lines. One looks in vain in Mailer's work for any comparable feeling about segregation. How angry that must make a writer like Baldwin, who feels it's a curse on the whole nation!

In an early essay on Harlem, Baldwin wrote of Negroes' ambivalent relations to Jews. "The Jew has been taught—and, too often, accepts—the legend of Negro inferiority; and the Negro, on the other hand, has found nothing in his experience

35

with Jews to counteract the legend of Semitic greed. Here the American white gentile has two legends serving him at once: he has divided these minorities and he rules. . . ." Baldwin sees the Jews caught in the "American crossfire," with the Negro hating the Jew not for his Jewishness but for the color of his skin. It was not the Jewish tradition by which he had been betrayed, but by the tradition of his native land. But just as a society must have a scapegoat, so hatred has to have a symbol. "Georgia has the Negro and Harlem has the Jew."

So, to Baldwin, Mailer belonged to a minority as he did, and also to a group that was traditionally hated in Harlem. Was there some feeling of this in Mailer's apparent escape from his background in Brooklyn? If so, he could escape only into the most hated group of all—the White. Nothing could let Mailer escape from being white; he was trapped for life. For blacks, he was on the other side, the oppressor, the enemy. On the one hand, he came from an oppressed race himself; on the other, he was saddled with a guilt complex that he could not overcome in the eyes of whites, however far he went along the path of the White Negro. One had the choice of being a rebel or a conformist—violent death threatening one, a stifling, cancerous death the other.

The Negro, doomed to live a life of constant humility or ever-threatening danger, became the rebel's—the hipster's—model. "The hipster had absorbed the existentialist synopses of the Negro, and for practical purposes could be considered a white Negro. . . ." So Mailer sought freedom from his minority role, his white guilt, by trying to cross over onto Baldwin's turf. No wonder *The White Negro* made Baldwin so angry. It would seem to him yet another example of the white man stealing the style and subject of the Negro when it was profitable. Mailer was attempting the reverse of Sammy Davis's claim to be a black Jew, and both were inviting psychic confusion and the risk of running away from acceptance of themselves. Did this confusion lie at the back of that stabbing incident, whatever had been the surface cause—liquor or drugs . . . ?

And if Baldwin saw Mailer as inescapably white and Jewish,

how had Mailer seen Baldwin in his evaluation of American writers? I looked at what he'd written. Baldwin, according to Mailer, was "too charming" a writer to be major. Even the best of his paragraphs were "sprayed with perfume." He was incapable of saying "Fuck you" to the reader. *Giovanni's Room* was a bad book, but mostly a brave one. Mailer—and was this the condescension that Baldwin had referred to?—said he itched at times to take a hammer to Baldwin's detachment, smash "the perfumed dome of his ego," and reduce him to what must be "one of the most tortured and magical nerves of our time." If Baldwin ever climbed the mountain, and really told it, we would have "the testament, and not a noble toilet water."

It was undoubtedly condescending, but also it was curiously unperceptive, coming from Mailer. There was one strange omission: reading Mailer's comments, you wouldn't have known Baldwin was black. A white liberal of the more sentimental kind might have thought this admirable, but surely it was impossible to assess Baldwin's courage as a writer without taking into account his position as a narrator of an unpopular cause and Boswell of the oppressed—for what a journey he had had to come himself before he could even address *anyone* else: Mailer or whoever. Mailer's attitude would have been more relevant if he had been examining the boy *he* had been. Would that nice Jewish kid have been capable of saying "Fuck you" to the reader?

One also gets an unpleasant notion from such words as "charming," "perfume," and "toilet water" that Mailer, reacting to the homosexual scenes in *Giovanni's Room,* was reflecting his own uneasy attitude toward homosexuality. At the time of *The Deer Park,* he had written that "my fear of homosexuality as a subject was stifling my creative reflexes," and even when he attempted to write about it with maximum tolerance in an essay entitled "The Homosexual Villain," he admitted that the result was "dressed in the gray of lugubrious caution." It was an essay that the nice boy in Brooklyn could have written. How then would Mailer react to a writer who dealt with the subject as freely as any other, for blacks grew up used

37

to being considered sex objects from every angle? Some of Mailer's "fear" seemed to show up in those "perfume" cracks; his piece about Baldwin was in fact like Baldwin's remarks about him—it told you even more about the writer than about the subject. When I brooded about both of them, only one thing seemed certain—black Negro and white Negro had thrown down the gauntlet to each other, declaring a kind of literary war, for remarks had been made that would be very hard to forgive. As if by mutual consent, Baldwin and I for the rest of that conversation got off the subject of Mailer and talked about the South. I'd been down there on a reporting trip, to follow the spread of desegregation and the battle over it—mob violence in New Orleans over school integration, brutal beatings over the right to eat at lunch counters in Atlanta. . . . I had stayed in one Southern city with a white businessman I had known in Europe, and whereas he had been articulately liberal in Europe, at home he was much more cautious. Baldwin gave a rueful smile when I told him about it. "That's one reason the South scares me so much," he said. "You never can be sure who will stand up and be counted—or if anyone will."

"I met a lot of whites who were risking the rage of their communities. I was told that Faulkner, in Oxford, Mississippi, had received threatening phone calls and some of his neighbors no longer speak to him . . ."

It was the wrong subject to bring up. Baldwin's face showed sudden anger, his eyes widening and his finger wagging as he said: "Faulkner's advice is to 'Go slow.' We've been told that for hundreds of years. How long are we supposed to go on going slow for the convenience of him and his fellow white Southerners? In an interview, Faulkner said that if it came to a contest between the federal government and Mississippi, he'd fight for Mississippi, even if it meant going out into the streets and shooting Negroes—"

I was foolish enough to try to turn back the torrent of Baldwin's rage. "Faulkner denied that that was what he said —or what he meant. Anyway I think his great books show clearly which side he is on. To write *Light in August* in about 1930—"

"I know all about his great books." Baldwin's tone now was ominously quiet and cold. "The highest tribute he could give Negroes in *The Sound and the Fury* after pages about whites was 'They endured,' as if they were capable only of that!"

"I think that's Faulkner's highest tribute to a human being—"

"Nonsense!" Baldwin cried. "Faulkner sanctifies that whole slave-holding society with a sort of romantic mystique full of references to Shiloh, Chickamauga, and Gettysburg. He won't give up his dreams of the past any more than any other white Southerner. But it's only when a man can surrender a dream that he sets himself free. Any real change means the break-up of the world as one has known it. That's the meaning of *Gone with the Wind.* But Faulkner wants to romanticize and maintain that grim reality."

I grumbled my disagreement—Faulkner was one of my heroes—but Baldwin wasn't listening. For him at that moment, Faulkner represented the South, not the South of out-and-out racism but the white liberalism he found weak and unreliable. His tone now was more confident, but also had a kind of public ring, as if he was beginning to think of himself as a spokesman who would be listened to. He had begun to supplement his income with some public speaking and he'd also started to travel in support of the civil rights movement. He had a new book of essays just out, *Nobody Knows My Name—More Notes of a Native Son,* and its subject matter and tone were much more militant and political than his earlier collection. He had included an essay about Mailer ("The Black Boy Looks at the White Boy"), which covered much of the same ground he had done in conversation with me. There was also a strong essay on "Faulkner and Desegregation." In the introduction, Baldwin said that something had ended for him: his youth, and also a certain attitude toward his color. "The question of who I was had at last become a personal question, and the answer

39

was to be found in me." The unexamined life was not worth living, as Plato had said; no writer could afford self-delusion "in the service of no matter what small or lofty cause." The question of color, he had come to realize, operated to hide the graver questions of the self. That was why the "Negro Problem" was so tenacious in American life—and so dangerous. But, he wrote, his own experience proved to him that the connection between American blacks and whites was "far deeper and more passionate than any of us like to think." The questions one asked oneself became one's key to the experience of others. "One could only face in others what one could face in oneself." What, I wondered, did that mean in personal terms of Mailer and Baldwin? What did the Brooklyn Jew and Harlem black have to face in themselves to appreciate the other?

Baldwin's new book also had three essays on Richard Wright under the general title of "Alas, Poor Richard." He recalled their first meeting in Brooklyn: "I was broke, naturally, shabby, hungry, and scared . . ." They became friends, then they had a row, a painful one because Wright meant so much to Baldwin—his work had been "an immense liberation and revelation." It was an argument over protest literature, Wright claiming that all literature was protest and Baldwin countering that all literature *might* be protest but all protest wasn't *literature.* They had tried without success to patch up the quarrel. Now, nearly twenty years had passed, and Richard Wright was dead. Baldwin had criticized him, but he didn't like others to do so. When an African with a small mocking laugh suggested that Richard Wright had thought he was white, Baldwin denied it—"I did not think I was white, either, or I did not *think* I thought so. But the Africans might think I did, and who could blame them? In their eyes, and in terms of my history, I could scarcely be considered the purest or most dependable of black men. . . ."

Baldwin's book was very well reviewed. *The Atlantic Monthly* called him "the voice of a new generation . . . a major literary talent" and it sold well throughout 1962 and then was a continuing best seller in paperback. His time had clearly come; he had found a popular audience. He had been luckier than Richard Wright in the timing of his birth; the civil rights movement provided him with a platform and a growing following. Very soon at this rate he would be as famous as Mailer.

I met Mailer briefly at his apartment in Brooklyn Heights. The room we were in had a magnificent view of the end of Manhattan and we sat facing it. Mailer appeared much more relaxed than when I'd last seen him, but the elder statesman manner was even more pronounced. On coming back to the U.S. he found he had profited from the respectful, forgiving English reception. The stabbing incident was fading into the past already; few journalists alluded to it now. He was on his way back to respectability if he didn't push out any further into more "extremes of experience." In talking with him, I had a strong impression he had come to a decision that he had gone as far as he should. Behind the self-confidence, there was still a little uneasiness, enough uncertainty about his future to keep him wary, cautious.

I had gone to see him to try to persuade him to write one of his long influential essays about a subject he hadn't touched: the young black militants down South. They traveled on shoe-strings, demonstrating against segregation with the panache of cavaliers, but there were rumors out of Congress that the old McCarthy witch-hunters were going to hold an investigation to try to prove they were all really Reds who should be suppressed. I fancied that an eloquent tribute from someone like Mailer might help to head off the investigation.

Mailer was at first interested, if a bit reluctant. He asked me if I could provide introductions and go with him to meet the people; he seemed almost shy about his possible reception. I said I would do anything I could to help. Then he suddenly backtracked, deciding that his name might do them more harm than good.

"I'm hardly respectable," he said with his self-deprecating grin.

Of course he was right; that was part of his appeal for many of his younger admirers. I mentioned his piece in *Esquire* about

41

Kennedy's nomination, "Superman Comes to the Supermarket." Something as persuasive as that would do a lot of good.

"Yes, but that was before . . ." his voice trailed away. Then: wasn't it more Jimmy Baldwin's kind of thing? he added with a widening smile of irony and perhaps a hint of mockery.

"Baldwin, being black, wouldn't be as persuasive with the white Establishment crowd—"

"And you think they would listen to *me?*" There was a tone of disbelief in his voice.

"You've got a big following."

He beamed; I was surprised he was still so sensitive about his popularity.

He refused to make any commitment then. He said he'd think about it and call me in the next couple of days. I never heard from him about it. The next time I met him he didn't mention it and neither did I. And he never wrote a piece. But then there was no witch-hunt either.

4

Twentieth Century, a quarterly magazine, decided to devote a whole issue to the topic of the times—violence. Among the aspects to be explored were crime, sports, violence on television and in movies. Inevitably Mailer was considered an authority and I was asked to interview him. It would be an opportunity, I thought, to get an answer to questions about the effects of his own "extremes of experience" that violence represented.

On the phone he seemed to welcome the chance to talk about it and he invited me to Brooklyn Heights. Before going, I wished to read over some account of what had happened on the night I suspected had changed his life. According to my Mailer file, the stabbing incident had occurred on November 19, 1960, and so I waded through back issues of *The New York Times,* but without success. I assumed I must have missed the report in the labyrinth of all those close columns, but an acquaintance of Mailer's claimed that the story had been late in reaching the public. Mailer, he said, must have had influence. Didn't I know that he had some powerful friends, like Sam Goldwyn? I'd met Sam Goldwyn in Hollywood, and though he'd come on more like a politician than a movie producer, I couldn't imagine his picking up the phone in Beverly Hills and calling whatever precinct Mailer had been taken to, or even getting a senator or a mayor to do it for him. I knew how long it sometimes took the police to work out what had happened in any row between a husband and wife; often, when they cooled down, neither wanted to talk against the other, and they treated the police like a common intruder or enemy. I remembered reading about the case in an international edition of *Time,* so I backtracked through issues of the magazine for November 1960. No luck. Eventually I found a big story in the December 5 issue, headed "Of Time and the Rebel," and complete with two pictures— one of a rather unkempt, unshaved Mailer pleading in Manhattan Felony Court with a burly, interested, and not unsympathetic cop standing behind him, and the other of a rather idealized, starry-eyed Mrs. Mailer.

At that time Mailer represented much of what *Time,* with its big business and conservative political interests, was actively against, so the magazine seemed to delight in his apparent downfall. Its story began with a prejudiced view of his career to date, detailing what it termed his "repeated failures"—first marriage ending in divorce, a Mexican marijuana kick, Seconal and Benzedrine in the Village ("he later managed to cure himself of dope"). *Time* saw him as a fiery advocate of "lost and leftist causes," an authority on hipsters, bebop, Marxism, existentialism, and even "in an excess of underdoggery" writing an article defending homosexuality, "an idea that revolted him." The magazine saw him making a "painful descent," with telltale signs of instability. He quarreled with his editors—*Time*'s editors seemed to assume an author must be in the wrong to do that—and his second marriage to Adele Morales, "a lush Peruvian-Spanish painter and actress," fluctuated, it said, from serenity in the morning to raging public brawls at night. He had had a brush with the police in Provincetown, it reported, when he hailed a prowl car under the impression it was a taxi, and in Birdland, the old Manhattan jazz hangout, there had been an argument over a check.

The scene was thus set for the *enfant terrible*'s undoing. Mailer held a party at his West Side Manhattan apartment; the two hundred guests included, according to *Time,* poets, prizefighters, homosexuals, writers, Big Beat Allen Ginsburg, actor Anthony Franciosa, *Commentary* editor Norman Podhoretz,

44

critic Delmore Schwartz, Syndicated Name Dropper Leonard Lyons. The host and hostess, the magazine reported, welcomed the guests in separate rooms, and as midnight passed, Mailer "drank deeply and became moodily belligerent." By the time the party broke up at 3:30 A.M., Mailer "had been in two fist fights, had received a small black eye."

Nearly five hours later, Adele Mailer checked into a downtown hospital "with critical wounds in her abdomen, her back and near her heart." By the time she had recovered enough to talk to detectives, her husband was said to be in a television studio, taping an interview with Mike Wallace. *Time* reported that he confirmed he intended to run for mayor of New York the next year on an existentialist ticket, and he also sounded off about juvenile delinquency, saying that it would not be solved by disarming young hoods: "The knife to a juvenile delinquent is very meaningful. You see, it's his sword—his manhood." Mrs. Mailer, after apparently saying on admission to the hospital that she had fallen on some broken glass, "admitted that her husband had stabbed her with a two-inch penknife soon after the party when she was preparing for bed." She said, according to *Time:* "He was depressed. He just came at me with a funny look in his eye. He didn't say a word. There was no reason. He just looked at me. Then he stabbed me." That night, the story went on, detectives found Mailer, neatly dressed and unshaven, sitting on a hospital bench near his wife's room.

In felony court a police psychiatrist urged that the writer be committed to a mental institution; he was "having an acute paranoid breakdown with delusional thinking, and [was] both homicidal and suicidal." *Time* said Mailer protested: "It is very important to me not to be sent to some mental institution. I'm a sane man. If this happens, for the rest of my life my work will be considered as the work of a man with a disordered mind. My pride is that as a sane man I can explore areas of experience that other men are afraid of. I insist I am sane." He was sent to Bellevue Hospital for mental observation.

The rebel, in *Time*'s account, seemed not only down but

nearly out. In an issue the following month, however, it reported that things were beginning to go right for him; was there a secret hope that the rebel had been tamed? He had been released from Bellevue as a sane man and his wife, the only witness, refused to file charges against him. She rejoined him at home. Feeling better, *Time* said, Mailer had even learned not to be a cop hater and it quoted *New York Post* columnist Murray Kempton as saying: "One of his surprises in his trouble has been the courtesy and sympathy of the police." A picture showed the Mailers together: Mrs. Mailer's arm through her husband's while he looked innocent and slightly bemused. A couple of issues later, Mailer had a letter in *Time,* saying: "Drear lads, I've never been a cop hater. Too small a role. But one is not a cop lover, for that is cancer gulch."

The *Time* story, of course, was reported from too rigid a viewpoint. It was instructive to compare the magazine's attitude at that time toward artists as opposed to businessmen and politicians; there was little delving into the corruption and mediocrity of so many of the latter, yet an intellectual adventurer like Mailer was treated not just with firm condescension but even outright disapproval. I would worry for Mailer when the magazine treated him with more respect; if that ever happened, either Mailer or the magazine would have radically changed attitudes toward the puzzle of living.

I flicked through the rest of that issue to get a feel again of those vanished days. The cover story dealt with Nigeria's Prime Minister Balewa; the letters column had suggestions for *Time*'s Man of the Year—1960; Caroline Kennedy and her father were seen in a picture taking a walk in Georgetown; Che Guevara was in Peking; the best sellers were *Advise and Consent* and *The Rise and Fall of the Third Reich;* in the movie columns, Ingmar Bergman's *The Virgin Spring* was reviewed.

It was all as much a part of history now as any other that had gone with the wind, but it was still close enough to remember the high hopes of that year as the comparatively young Kennedy prepared to take over from the aging Eisenhower and the civil rights movement was beginning to seem relevant to

46

everybody. It is the fashion now to criticize Kennedy after the years of Camelot adulation, but that time at least brought an increase in tolerance. People began to talk more about what they wanted to *do* with their lives, rather than seeking either conformity or security at any price. It seemed to me that Norman Mailer had been lucky to have reached his most far-out experience, certainly his riskiest, at this time rather than, say, in the more intolerant fifties.

He looked in good shape when I met him for the *Twentieth Century* interview—far from the rumpled figure in the *Time* photograph. Mellow, his weight under control, he was as well groomed as a successful politician—and he looked more Irish than ever.

We sat in his apartment facing the panoramic view of down-town Manhattan through the huge window, and watched the sun go down between the skyscrapers. We talked briefly of two recent deaths: Marilyn Monroe's and Hemingway's. Hemingway's was, of course, suicide, but no one seemed sure whether Monroe's had been an accident or suicide; there were even rumors of murder, though I attributed this to the plague of paranoia sweeping the country—people saw plots and conspiracies behind everything. I had known Marilyn Monroe; Mailer said he hadn't, but he knew her ex-husband, dramatist Arthur Miller, slightly. He seemed to grow impatient as I talked about her and switched the subject back to Hemingway.

"He was our greatest living romantic," Mailer declared. "He knew the value of his own work and he fought to let his personality enrich that work. He pushed out into the extremities of new experience until he became popular and then, like a politician, he grew afraid of losing his popularity. But he remained a challenge to conformity—bureaucracy will cheer at his death! But his suicide by the gun is fitting; he had been with guns since he was a young boy. It represented another extreme experience, blowing himself into eternity . . ."

Hemingway had been a father figure for Mailer the writer and now he left a vacuum that Mailer perhaps hoped to fill.

47

Hemingway, too, had a reputation as a student of violence—he had been involved in public brawls. Mailer perhaps was already measuring himself as Hemingway's successor, "America's Greatest Living Writer." There would be contenders but Mailer had already dealt with them in *Advertisements for Myself.* Baldwin was "too charming a writer to be major." James Jones should give up "the lust to measure his talent by the money he makes." William Styron was "not nearly as big as he ought to be." Truman Capote at his worst "has less to say than any good writer I know." He couldn't take Saul Bellow seriously as a major novelist. And so on. Only one writer seemed to be left at the end as heavyweight champ—Mailer himself. It was a good example of Mailer's aggressive side. He made a reference to all the fights he'd been in, all the bruises and black eyes, and he was clearly proud of it, admitting the reason for it in that way people found so charming—"I was a physical coward as a child." Perhaps that nice, sensitive Jewish boy hadn't liked to fight; he had forced himself to change by walking into fights the way some army heroes walked into battle; his wounds were the answer to his early fear of cowardice and he still collected them, turning aggressive in a flash that sometimes apparently bewildered even close friends.

He had warmed up enough now for the interview. An interviewer can do violence to a reputation simply by quoting verbatim, by serving up the matter with none of the manner. An old victim of this kind of journalistic violence, Mailer was wary of being caught again. "I'd be grateful if you'd tell how I said it as well as what I said," he told me. I understood his point when I read my notes afterward. What might seem in verbatim like a speech was more often a thought slowly and wryly trapped, sometimes more like musing aloud than being interviewed.

I asked him for his definition of violence; people used the word like "love" in so many conflicting ways.

Mailer leaned toward me, his broad shoulders slightly hunched as he coaxed out the words.

"Well, it seems to me there are two kinds, and they are altogether different. One is personal violence: an act of violence by a man or a woman against other men or women." He looked at me as if daring me to make any personal references. I kept quiet. "The second kind is social violence: concentration camps, nuclear warfare. If one wants to carry the notion far enough, there are subtler forms of social violence, such as censorship, or excessively organized piety, or charity drives. Social violence creates personal violence as its antithesis. A juvenile delinquent is violent not because his parents were necessarily violent to him nor even because society is directly violent to him—he's not, let's say, beaten in school—but because his spontaneous expressions are cut off by institutional deadenings of his nature. The boy who lives in a housing project is more likely to be violent than the same boy living in a slum tenement because the housing project puts him in direct contact with a deadening environment. The housing project is not a neighborhood but a massive barracks . . ."

He was frowning with concentration—Mailer the philosopher. Shades of Harvard! I was disappointed that he was generalizing, dealing in the abstract instead of the personal. "Violence is directly proportional to the power to deaden one's mood, which is possessed by the environment. Threatened with the extinction of our possibilities, we react with chronic rage. Violence begins, you see, as the desire to fight one's way out of a trap. Moral questions over the nature of one's violence come only as a secondary matter. The first reaction, the heart of the violence, is the protection of the self. The second question, the moral question, is whether the self deserves to be protected, that is to say—was it honorable to fight? Was the danger true? For example, if a boy beats up an old woman, he may be protecting himself by discharging a rage which would destroy his body if it were left to work on the cells, so he takes it out on the old woman. The boy may be anything from a brute to Raskolnikov. It requires an exquisite sense of context and a subtle gift as a moralist to decide these matters at times. Mexicans have a saying that when you commit murder, you carry the dead man's soul on your back, and you have to work not only for one soul then, but for two souls . . ."

49

Was that the way he saw himself in the early morning after that party—"discharging a rage which would destroy his body . . ."?

Mailer's mind, or at least his words, were far from such considerations; he couldn't have been more impersonal.

"It does seem more or less self-evident," he said, "that men who have lived a great deal with violence are usually gentler and more tolerant than men who abhor violence. Boxers, bullfighters, a lot of combat soldiers, Hemingway heroes, in short, are almost always gentle men. It is not because they have read Hemingway. They were gentle long before Hemingway was born. It is just that Hemingway was the first writer who observed the repetition of this fact and paid his profound respects to it.

"I think the reason is that men who are otherwise serious but ready for personal violence—"

Ah! He had my whole attention now.

"—are almost always religious. They have a deep sense of dread, of responsibility, of woe, of reluctance to make an error in violence—and a grim, almost tragic sense of how far violence can carry them. If I think of the athletes, criminals, and prizefighters I've known, and the Negroes living in Harlem—whose lives have much in common with athletes, criminals and prizefighters—they all have an understanding of life which is comprehensive and often tragic. It is, of course, deadeningly void of any kind of culture which could sustain them in their more boring times, but they do have a specific gravity and a depth of compassion which one doesn't find in their social opposite, the university-trained intellectuals . . ."

I caught a glimpse of why Baldwin disliked *The White Negro* so much; this pigeonholing of Negroes among criminals, athletes and prizefighters might have some intellectual justification, but would be resented nevertheless by the people themselves, who would see it as an attempt to put them down. Mailer saw the Negro as born to extremes of experience by the very nature of his place in society. Whereas he himself had to seek it, Baldwin had that sort of experience thrust upon him.

There was a danger then that Baldwin would pull rank—perhaps on that account he was best kept at a distance; any encounter might be uneven, unfair.

Edging up on this point, I asked Mailer if he thought the university-trained intellectual was too protected.

He responded with great diplomacy. "It's not that he is protected from violence—although of course he is—so much as that he is not in contact with existential experience. I mean experience sufficiently unusual so that you don't know how it is going to turn out. You don't know whether you're going to be cheered or derided at the end of it, wanted or rejected, dead or alive. Now obviously there are few experiences which can by these rigorous terms be called existential. But the hoodlum is more likely to encounter existential experience than the university man."

He looked very thoughtful, perhaps remembering—surely memory signaled. "Something happens in an act of violence which is beyond one's measure. If a bully is beating up a friend who is smaller than himself and knows precisely the point at which he is going to quit, that's not really an act of violence. That's simply excretion. That's why we despise the bully. But when violence is larger than one's ability to dominate—"

Ah, yes.

"—it is existential, and one is living in an world of instantaneous revelations. The saint and the psychopath share the same kind of experience. It is just that the saint has the mysterious virtue of being able to transcend this experience and the psychopath is broken or made murderous."

I tried a different tack to bring him to the personal. How did his view of violence relate to our own time?

"I wouldn't call the twentieth century a violent period so far as personal violence goes. It is a time of plague. When people sense that pestilence is upon them, however, they *tend* to be violent. The powerful impulse of the twentieth century has been to defeat this tendency by elaborate social institutions which destroy the possibility of personal violence before it can have a free expression. Just for example—psychoanalysis, Police Athletic Leagues, wars on juvenile delinquency, watered revolutions, Fabianism, our 'War on Poverty.' The notion, finally, that if individual feelings are discouraged at every turn and social irritations are blanketed by benefits and welfare programs, then the desire to reach toward one's own individual feelings as a solution becomes stupefied.

"The impulse of the twentieth century seems to be a desire to make society run on rails. Anything may be tolerated, even communism, provided that the dialectic is squeezed out of our nature. So the dramatic acts of violence in the twentieth century . . ." He paused momentarily to come up with examples —the deposition of Khrushchev, Hemingway's suicide, the Chinese setting off their atomic bomb, the Yankees firing Yogi Berra; examples began to crowd in upon him as he gave it thought. "These are all expressions of the social suffocations of the twentieth century. These acts demonstrate that there is something in the center of nature itself which resists any social directive that life not be complex, not be perverse, not contradictory, not explosive, not full of ambush and reward. Romance may be the center of existence. But once romance is suffocated by our modern vision of society, a vision now more mechanical than the most monotonous of machines, violence becomes the child of romance."

Mailer was preoccupied now with one of his pet obsessions. "The very materials of our world suffocate us everywhere. A perfect example—the technological signature of the twentieth century—is plastic: material without any grain, any organic substance, any natural color or predictability. Yet reasonable predictability, after all, is the armature on which great societies in the past have been built. Plastic, however, cracks in two for no reason whatsoever. It bears up under killing punishments and then suddenly explodes in the night. A fiber glass hull can go through storms which would spring a leak in a wooden hull. Then, one day, in a modest squall, the fiber glass splits completely. Or abruptly capsizes. That's because it is a material which is not even divorced from nature but indeed has not ever *been* a part of nature. Plastic is the perfect metaphor for twentieth century man—and for the curious, stupefying, bewildering nature of much modern violence.

"Our obsession with violence comes, I think, not because its daily incidence is so high but because we are suffocated and so *think* constantly of violence. Can one argue seriously that our streets are less safe to walk on than the streets of Paris in 1300? Or Naples in 1644? But the twentieth century, in destroying a romantic view of existence, has created an awareness of violence as electric as paranoia."

Did this apply to writing—the arts?

He thought carefully before replying. "There was a time when an artist could feel respectable about being a naturalist. Zola, Ibsen, Shaw were heroes. So were de Maupassant, Dreiser, Farrell. Our realists were heroes; so were our novelists of manners, like Henry James. The natural work of a good artist is to try to write or discover what it is all about. Realism was a way of moving into this mystery just as manners was a way. But there has been so much work done that violence appeals to the artist now because it is the least tangible, the least explored frontier. It's exceptionally difficult to write about."

Was that because it so easily became melodrama?

"Describing the aftermath of violence," he said, "is not difficult because it takes you back into realism. Of course if you don't do it well enough, you're marooned in melodrama. If you do it superbly, you're writing about manners. But it *is* difficult to write about violence in the act because—like love—while you are experiencing it, you can't observe it. You lose your professional consciousness. Heisenberg's principle of uncertainty is in the wings. If you observe an action, the action is affected by the observation. Now, perhaps such emotions as love can be recorded truly—one's memory returns the truth. One can remember in entirety meeting a woman with whom one was once in love, and so be able to write about it. A number of sentimental memories can be recorded truly. An act of violence, however, cannot be recorded truly because the action did not create a mood but shattered a series of moods. So to write about violence is always an act of creation. One must make up an act of violence in order to write about it."

I wondered if we were touching on any of the root causes of the incident that night—could he have been "making up" an act of violence? He was talking on and I wouldn't have asked even if he hadn't been; I felt he wanted to keep it all on a general, abstract level.

"The marvelous thing Hemingway did at his best was to show that the only way to begin to write about half the important matters on earth was to create the mood, or the destruction of mood, in which they occurred—rather than try to establish the truth of the event. It is possible that his years as a reporter inspired him with a passion for such emotional accuracy since he knew that the onerous duty of a journalist is to replace the mood by the fact and so create one kind of history, a fictional history, in opposition to the violent—that is, palpable—actuality of the event."

I was making one last attempt to tie him down to the personal. "You mean the writer's preoccupation with violence today arises not so much from the climate of the times as from his knowledge of his craft and what remains to be achieved?"

"When I talked earlier," he said, "about the collective sense of pending violence which has hovered over the twentieth century—and which became so real at the time of the concentration camps—I suppose what I was trying to say is that violence is not something we have to worry about in a real sense from day to day. We worry about it when that part of ourselves which is paranoid attempts to foresee the consequences of our collective suffocation. The average twentieth-century man lives a life more physically secure than ever before, at least in these immediate years, but as we also have our collective sense of oncoming plague, the artist, more sensitive to tendency than to actuality, becomes obsessed with violence. Just as many a man no longer has a sense of his home as his castle and often conceives himself as more safe on his job, more nurtured, than at home—at least so far as psychic warfare goes—well, perhaps for that reason the artist, good and bad alike, has discovered that the most incisive way to reach an audience is through violence in his work, through the sober presentation of violent people in violent acts or through a violent presentation of sober people in sober acts—satire."

Mailer leaned back and relaxed, winding it all up. "The phenomenon of satirical books like *Candy* is that they are usually modest works—*Naked Lunch* would be a thunderous exception—with a mild sense of satire more like firecrackers than claws, and void of any moral nuance, yet they're merry works—*Catch-22,* for example—and curiously decent. They bring balm to the tortured. There's something near to heavenly about them, as if God had said, 'You poor tortured little devils, all full of pus, you need something ferocious, malicious, to aid your constipation. Glad to give it to you. Here's some Candy.' Of course, all the sober sticks like myself are trying to do the opposite—violent people in violent acts brought back alive to realism. Either way, the interest in violence brings literature closer to athletics—we want to break records. It's not the worst atmosphere for literature; just about democratic, if you think of it."

The interview was over; my chance was gone unless the really personal answers were already there between the lines. We chatted and I remember Baldwin's name came up once. Mailer said Baldwin had once gone out on a limb where blacks and whites meet, where blacks get lynched and whites meet the fate of traitors.

Wasn't Baldwin still out there?

"Fame's hitting Jimmy now," Mailer said. "He'll get it the way I did with *The Naked and the Dead.* It'll change his life; he may not be able to take it."

We went on to talk about some of Mailer's other interests, safer ones—architecture, the cure for cancer. . . .

The next day he phoned to say he'd awakened worried that he'd used a lot of words but said little, not what he meant. And so I provided him—unwillingly—with my notes typed out. I had once done that for the English novelist Anthony Powell, and he took out every colloquial, slangy expression he'd used in our interview; undoubtedly he sharpened his meaning, but at the expense of his tone, his individual expression and all that it reflected. I didn't want Mailer doing the same, but I didn't have much choice.

For a couple of days Mailer brooded over the typescript. When he sent it back, I found he had inserted one fresh paragraph and clarified many of the sentences; he changed a word in one of my questions and sent me an apology for taking what he called "the liberty." This care over even an interview, over what he released to the world, made me think of an artist of great integrity—or a politician worried about his image. As with everyone, it depended on how you saw him.

5

I hadn't known Baldwin in Europe during the years of struggle, but now the tide was turning for him; I met him there by chance and found him subtly freer and more relaxed than he had been in New York. He was obviously able to shed some of his deepest responsibilities and concerns, however much he might insist in his essays that he took himself and his blackness wherever he went. Europe might be predominantly white, like the United States, but Baldwin's own identity changed—he was no longer an insider, he was no longer just black; he was an outsider first, then an American, and then black; it was an identity he obviously enjoyed.

I had gone to the island of Majorca to cover the awarding of the Prix Formentor. It was a newly established prize but received a lot of attention because it was worth over $10,000. Literary prizes generally amount to no more than a medal and the price of dinner. An international group of publishers was behind the prize—the winning author's book would be published simultaneously in about a dozen languages. Delegations of judges came from a number of countries, all expenses paid.

On arrival on the beautiful rocky Mediterranean island, I was glad to learn that Baldwin was to be part of the American delegation, because it was some time since I'd seen him and a lot was happening both with the civil rights movement and with him. But by the start of the first session, with all the delegations plugging particular candidates, Baldwin still hadn't arrived. I remembered him back in his Horatio Street apartment with his one suit; now he was well enough known and meeting enough of the right people to get invitations to junkets like this one. The organizers were confident he would arrive; remembering Detroit, I was less sure. The second day came and went. The organizers sent a car to the airport to pick him up but he wasn't on the plane. The American delegation was now anxious; a strong personality on their side was badly needed. The Italians were assuming a dominant role, and maybe Baldwin, who was both black and could speak French as forcefully as he could speak English—two aces—could redress the balance.

Whenever literary people, writers and critics, are overly righteous about politicians, I remember that Majorca conference. I had traveled with some members of the British delegation. They seemed very keen to make sure that the Australian writer, Patrick White, didn't snatch the prize away from one of their candidates. The biggest threat, however, was from the Italian delegation, for it included that superb diplomat, Alberto Moravia, who was pushing his own candidate. The British hoped that Angus Wilson, smiling and friendly and very shrewd, would be their answer to Moravia. Who was plugging the best writer seemed irrelevant; the aim was to win. It was all good political fun.

The American delegation's influence had been weakened because not all the members had read the works nominated, especially those from Europe and Asia that were untranslated. After Henry Miller came down with influenza, Harvey Breit became chief spokesman, and he admitted often, quite openly and honestly, his ignorance of some of the writers being considered. It caused some of the more cynical Europeans to shrug their shoulders at this latest example of American Innocence. It was giving the more wily British and Italians too easy an advantage; the prize was clearly within the grasp of the delegation of either Angus Wilson or Alberto Moravia. Only a strong contribution from the missing Baldwin (as strong as those renunciations of the devil when he was a boy preacher) could turn the tables now. He kept promising to arrive. . . .

I talked with the two men whom the others were trying to set up as rival Machiavellis. My money was on Moravia. Angus Wilson didn't seem to have an intense enough will to win; he went around beaming like one's favorite uncle, and he even spoke well of Patrick White, to the dismay of those Britons who were still fearful the Australian writer would carry off the prize. Moravia had a much more dedicated and ambitious attitude. He talked about his candidate like a presidential campaign manager wooing voters; I'm sure if there had been a baby present, he would gladly have kissed it. He walked with a slight limp, his gentle eyes in conflict with his jutting jaw; he reminded me of an Italian Charles Boyer, at a time when American matrons thought middle-aged European men with foreign accents were romantic figures. He first of all spoke as the literary craftsman. Third-person narrative belonged to a period when people believed in objective reality. Nowadays we believed mostly in subjective reality—"Everybody is his own reality and your reality is not mine." In his recent books he had tried to write about the—how did we say it in English?—"the lower people."

"Do you mean lower in a class sense?"

"I mean the working people. . . ."

He also talked business, and then I could see why he had such a formidable reputation as a literary diplomat. He was pushing a novel about a teenaged girl in Rome, *The Age of Malaise,* by a young Italian woman named Dacia Maraini. He introduced her name into the conversation very quietly, very slyly, and then proceeded to press her claim to the prize: "She is very modern and has much talent. She is also very pretty—and that is very important in life, yes? By modern, I mean she was born with some of the quality which modern writers sometimes acquire artificially . . ."

Miss Maraini seemed no more outstanding than a dozen other writers who might have been nominated, but listening to Moravia's charming determination, I had a feeling that she would inevitably get the prize. Where the hell was Baldwin?

He arrived at last, close to the end, making a sudden dramatic entrance. He was sorry to be late, but—and his mouth widened in a happy, gap-toothed grin—he'd been detained at the White House. Kennedy was courting artists to give his administration a little cultural tone; Faulkner had turned down an invitation, saying it was too far to go to eat with strangers; but Baldwin was clearly delighted. From Harlem to the White House! It was even better than the old white claim—from log cabin to the White House. Not bad for a nigger, huh? his pleased expression seemed to say as the other delegates applauded him.

He looked sleeker, better dressed, even a little heavier, though he was still as slight as a sparrow. Moravia had the confident air of someone born to success, an Italian intellectual secure in every way—an aristocrat! A Harlem boy couldn't hope to rival all those years of good living, but Baldwin had something that in its way was even better for the ego: the old Cinderella overnight trip from rags to riches. If big money hadn't arrived yet, it was on its way; the civil rights movement was sweeping him to fame. It was like being on the crest of a gigantic wave: it might take him anywhere. Nothing he could do now, even if he wanted to, could bring back his privacy. American overnight success could be stunning, but Baldwin wouldn't see it that way; he would recall those grim years of struggle uptown and here in Europe, and it would seem long enough in coming. To a Richard Wright he would have seemed fantastically lucky in the timing of his birth.

Yet the changes were apparently outward; alone over a drink, we might have been back on Horatio Street. Amid the applauding international publishers and their secretaries, the organizers, the established like Moravia, a familiar face seemed extremely welcome; perhaps Baldwin was looking for a sign that his life had changed but he had not. He shook off some of the hangers-on and we retired to a corner of the hotel with strong drinks.

"You've become famous, Jimmy."

"It's all a load of bullshit . . ." He touched me quickly on the arm as if asking me to believe him.

"You seem different, less tense."

"I haven't changed!" He was almost angry. Then he smiled. "Do you think I've been through all I've been through, paid the dues, to be impressed by . . . this! Publishers are business people; they have screwed me every way there is. At first I couldn't get published, then when they saw money in me they gave me a few pennies. Of course you meet exceptions. That's the heart of life—exceptions! There's always one, whether he's a businessman or someone white, whose life prevents you from that all-embracing generalization, from making a complete rejection.

"So you've got to be careful. No, if I seem changed or less tense, it's more likely to be the effect of being away, of being back in Europe. It's a battleground at home now; I feel like a soldier on furlough. And it's going to get worse. As we test the enemy all along the line—at lunch counters, restaurants, on the job, at school—the level of violence will inevitably rise." The prospects ahead seemed to depress him; too many people might have to risk their lives. He tried to check his grim vision, his fierceness, by turning to reminiscence. "I remember my astonishment when I first came to Europe and discovered I was as American as any white Texan cowboy. I had left America because I doubted that I could survive the fury of color prejudice there; now I know if I don't survive it, I won't survive at all. . . ."

We decided to leave the hotel bar and stroll outside in the warm night. There were no lights in the hotel grounds, the darkness seemed total beneath the trees, and I couldn't even see Baldwin's silhouette; I could only hear him above the hum of insects—that intense, nervous voice.

"I used to feel totally alone, as isolated from my own people as I was from whites. I was in danger of believing what whites said about me. *That* is what I have been through, and now I intend to be compensated for it. I remember when I first came to Europe I listened to some of my heritage—like Bessie Smith

—in a way I had never done in America. And that helped reconcile me to being a nigger. It released me from my hatred. I don't hate those violent whites back home; I'm sorry for them in the deepest sense. They have destroyed their own humanity. But how long can I afford to feel sorry? The way things are going, kids beaten up and jailed, we'll all be lucky not to drown in hatred.

"Coming to Europe," he added, his voice more gentle, "also freed me as a writer. We don't take writers seriously back home. I was a double weirdo: black *and* a writer. Europeans, being so much older, have at least learned that writers are a fact of life and put up with them. In Europe I could mix at all levels of society in a way that was impossible for me in America, and I love to talk to people—"

"Mailer recently told me how restricted he found American society. Vast areas of experience he couldn't get near."

"He was exaggerating. As a white, he had it easy compared to someone like me. Jews exaggerate the trouble they run into in America to hide the fact that they own large parts of the goddam country. And Norman can't bear to think he had it easy any more than any other white liberal. But, baby, it's not your time now; it's our time; and if you want to be in on the action, you'll have to play second fiddle. Norman doesn't like that role. But he, like all writers—but he's *particularly* prone to it—will have to be careful he doesn't allow the fantasy structure we all create around ourselves to become a prison instead of a fortress."

"I felt that was what he'd allowed to happen at the time of that stabbing incident."

"You sometimes have to burn down the house to escape from it. Adele and Norman have since got divorced. I used to enjoy them together—there was a great sense of life, of enjoyment. Norman was one of those people who helped me to overcome some of my tough-guy lack of charity. I was so far gone I could never accept that white people had real trouble. But of course Norman and I couldn't really meet on equal terms. It wasn't anything to do with color—though Norman has his hang-ups.

62

"But he accepted that myth of the sexuality of Negroes so many whites refuse to give up. If you had washed as many dirty diapers as I did when I was helping my mother to bring up the rest of the kids, if you'd lived with all the funkiness I have, you'd roar with laughter, too, over that great big white myth of Negro sexuality. It only comes from the whites' puritanical hang-ups about their own sex. To put it bluntly, some black women are great in bed, some are not, some black men have big dicks, some don't. Where the Negro is unique is in a kind of beauty. They are a very beautiful people—*we* are a very beautiful people—and I'm not talking about sex at all. How many Negroes despair of whites because inevitably, as if they're obeying some Newtonian physical law, any conversation with them sooner or later gets down to sex. I bet you're a great lay. I bet you're great in bed. Fuck bed! There's more to life than that, baby, but you want to stick us with only that. Even a very perceptive man like Norman falls for that bullshit, that White Negro bullshit. The whites are creating fantasies about Negro sexuality while what we're wondering in our urine-stained hallways is what will happen to the beauty we see all around us, the beauty of our brothers and sisters, our buddies? Will it be corrupted, destroyed? That's what the fight's about. We have absolutely nothing to lose. But that wasn't what kept Norman and me apart. It was more that he was flushed with success and I was full of a sense of failure—"

"Maybe now it would be easier—"

"No, I don't think so. In a subtle way, the roles have been reversed. I've now been given an activist role, one that Norman's color prevents him from having, and since he has that Hemingway obsession about the writer as man of action, he probably envies me now in the same troubled way I used to envy him."

"Maybe he'll find a role for himself—maybe he'll run for mayor."

"Not yet. He hasn't really won back his respectability, though the American people who have very short memories, are incredibly fickle. That's why it's so hard to get through to

63

them now. They expect us to have short memories, too; to forget lynching and slavery and segregation and all the other variations on the same theme of cruelty and greed. White liberals, for all their guilt, are simply embarrassed if we show any real anger—the eye-for-an-eye kind. They're always wanting you to be reasonable, to turn the other cheek. Fuck the other cheek—"

"Do you remember when Mailer wrote that you seemed incapable of saying 'Fuck you' to the reader, though in those days he felt bound to write it as F—— you?"

"Could I ever forget it? Now that I'm on the barricades, he probably sees me differently. Norman in many ways is full of illusions. What we're going through is to awaken white intellectuals like him as much as anyone else. They fool themselves they know us. They don't know us at all. At all! I remember Negro jazz musicians in Paris in the old days; they really liked Norman, they did, but they did not consider him at all hip, at least those I knew. But whites like Norman have a great role if they will only accept that it's secondary. They can't be the stars, they can't lead *us,* for God's sake, but we need them if the racial nightmare is to end and we are all to wake up in time. The future—and it's taken a long time for me to accept this —really depends on blacks and whites, those who are awake already, conscious already, helping like lovers to create the consciousness of others. Norman and I have a duty to come together, to understand each other, to try to overcome the competitive sense this society creates to keep us apart."

"Do you think that's any more possible than Mailer's accepting a secondary role?"

Baldwin didn't have a chance to reply; somewhere over to our left a man's voice called through the darkness: "Mr. Baldwin! . . . Mr. Baldwin! . . ."

We still couldn't see each other; the caller was just a voice somewhere in the black night.

"I'm here," Baldwin called back.

We all tried to find each other. Eventually we saw a narrow beam of light; the man looking for Baldwin had taken the precaution of bringing a flashlight with him.

It was someone connected with the organizers; the publishers were missing the new celebrity. Baldwin sighed; would I excuse him for a few minutes? "I've got to remember they're paying the bill and I'm expected to sing for my supper," he said.

I went back to my hotel room to write a story for a newspaper about the conference. There wasn't much to say yet—the big session would be in the morning; Baldwin had arrived just in time for that. I went over my notes about what Moravia had said. After the Second World War, he'd recalled, even the rich had suffered from hardship, though "the poor were paying for everybody, as usual." That was a line that would have appealed to Baldwin—perhaps the starting point, where you crossed the line between black and white, was among the poor. Yet in the United States the white poor were among the most prejudiced, seeing the Negroes as rivals for the unskilled jobs, trying to bolster up their own pride by seeing Negroes as inferior. Was this where whites like Mailer could perhaps do their finest work —showing up the poor whites' illusions? Could a writer have any effect?

The poor of any color didn't buy books. Was this what bugged Mailer? Baldwin had found his platform, he didn't need books to reach *his* audience, but where was Mailer's platform? I read over again what Moravia had said about subjective reality: "The first-person narrative is better than the third person for me. The third person is too artificial because it gives the impression the writer is omniscient." Baldwin certainly had the same attitude in his work; everything became subjective, a matter of personal experience. Mailer swung between the approach summed up by *Advertisements for Myself* and more generalized arguments that seemed to belong to the old Harvard man.

Both approaches had extreme dangers; the subjective always threatening to explode in a kind of egocentric madness and the generalized argument verging always on too much abstraction, a kind of easy intellectual and personal security. "Everybody is his own reality and your reality is not mine," Moravia had said. "But it could be I will go back sometime to write in the third person. My face changes, I change, and perhaps my books change. . . ." We were in a fantastic period of change, Mailer and Baldwin had both gone through changes in the comparatively short time I'd watched them, and no doubt great changes were ahead. For them, for us all.

I saw Baldwin late that night in the hotel bar. He seemed pretty high, a big glass of Scotch at his elbow, and he was being wooed by one of the publishers who wanted Baldwin to switch to him. It was like a cat-and-mouse act, though I fancied Baldwin was not as innocent and starry-eyed as he came on. He was playing a game of his own that he was enjoying. It must have made a pleasant change to be courted so enthusiastically after the years of rejection, the Horatio Street obscurity, and then the small advances. He deserved some fun at a publisher's expense.

The next day the politicians, the lobbyists, the literary strategists faced each other in the final confrontation over that $10,000 prize. The American delegation put Baldwin forward. He made an impassioned, finger-wagging speech in favor of Katherine Anne Porter; he couldn't have done better when he was a boy preacher. But his eloquence, the strength of his personality, were no match for the days and nights of old-fashioned persuasion. The cynical, sophisticated Europeans applauded, nodded, and smiled, but they had already made up their minds—or had them made up for them by that expert in subjective realism. Moravia's candidate was the winner.

Then it was all over: I remember the early-morning departures. Moravia with a justifiable look of triumph, Baldwin and Angus Wilson exchanging friendly greetings. "No wonder," Baldwin said quietly to me, "that American writers still run off to Europe. In this decadent continent there is a strange kind of peace we're too young to know. Europe has lived long enough to learn the inexorable limits of life—that it all ends in tragedy. And we have that youthful quality that Europe has lost—a sense of life's possibilities, that you can change things for the better if you have the determination. The two really should go hand-in-hand if we are to progress. But I can only find them by straddling both continents. And that is why I shall have to go home shortly . . . and yet when I get there, immediately plan when I'm coming back here. We need to wed the vision of the Old World and the New into one society, a society realizing the intangible dreams of people." He looked at the beautiful early-morning sky. "That is what is happening at home now—people are trying to put their dreams into reality. It will be wonderful if they succeed, but a nightmare if they don't."

6

I also watched Norman Mailer perform at an international writers' conference—in Edinburgh. He was also late arriving. It wasn't because of the White House—ah, how that would have warmed his political ambitions!—but because his new wife was having a baby. He had married Lady Jeanne Campbell, a British journalist who was the daughter of the Duke of Argyll and granddaughter of Lord Beaverbrook, the newspaper owner and politician.

When I met Mailer this time, he came on with an imitation of a lofty English accent. Maybe his new wife spoke that way, but I couldn't believe it. It was more like the way P.G.Wodehouse's characters spoke to their butlers. Perhaps that was Mailer's view of Britain—or of London, however much he had seen of that complex island—for he grinned wickedly, as if he was stripping bare the ancient snobberies. I had met his new wife once when, as reporters, we were both covering the same event, and I remembered she had a much more earthy accent. Mailer perhaps was responding to his feelings about her title or to the kind of English people he might meet with her at her father's dukedom. His marriage certainly gave him the key to classes in Britain he could never get near at home. How he must have wanted to shake it in the face of those snotty New York society hostesses who had never invited him or who had crossed him off after the stabbing incident! Let even Jackie Kennedy brood over it, for hadn't she invited the safe talents, but never him, or those like him, who were taking risks (and were therefore risky)? Why would Saul Bellow and J.D.Salinger make it —as he had claimed in an essay—"long before William Burroughs or Norman Mailer"? But perhaps marriage to a titled English woman was worth more socially than an old scandal. Surely Mailer the politician could be grateful for once to Mailer the romantic: this was one love match that might help. So let him tarry in the U.S. while his wife labored; his appearance in Edinburgh could be postponed a day or two without losing its value.

The conference missed his presence as Formentor had missed Baldwin's. Angus Wilson was there, but no Alberto Moravia. Mailer wasn't the only absentee. Regrets poured in with every mail delivery. International gatherings of writers are so rare that there is no adequate word to describe them; someone at the start suggested a "riot" of writers might do as a collective noun if the writers lived up to their reputations; but as the casualty list grew, it seemed as if an "absence" of writers might be more accurate. Messages of regret arrived from the garrets and the plush suites of Europe and America, from writers ill or preoccupied or expecting babies or novels or just running true to form and being temperamental. If this had gone on long enough, the doors of Edinburgh's McEwan Hall would have opened on an empty platform except for John Calder, the publisher and organizer of the conference, and Malcolm Muggeridge, the chairman. Happily enough, stragglers turned up to prove that writers *can* keep appointments and stand each other's company, at least for a few hours, and a long line of gawkers outside was let in to have a look at them.

None of the organizers announced who had turned up and who had not, so the massed readers in the audience were left to try to relate the faces before them to the books they had read. The usually out-of-date pictures on book jackets were clearly not much help and only a few writers spoke up to be identified by Mr. Muggeridge. Luckily Mary McCarthy was the second speaker, and several hundred fans waited for her to justify her reputation as the most devastating of writer-critics. She obligingly smoked her cigarette like a stiletto, working up tension as to whom she might stab next, and then took a hearty lunge at Angus Wilson's claim that the English novel was healthily using traditional forms with an overlay of irony. Oh, she didn't agree with that; not at all. Stab, stab, stab. The corpses of reputations and of books soon littered the platform.

Among those listening to her were Henry Miller, looking as lean as a retired cowboy—Gary Cooper's father perhaps—and his old buddy, Lawrence Durrell, as cheerful and overweight as a businessman dining on credit cards; they kept giving each other the sly looks of old friends. Miller eventually rose to pronounce the novel dead and express the hope that the conference would soon get down to discussing more relevant arts such as painting and music.

The local Scottish writers created the most excitement in noisily resisting English, European, and American influences. Mailer's new daughter, Kate, had been delivered by this time, and he made a modest entrance while the Scots were hard at it. Mailer seemed suitably impressed by the verbal violence of the Scots. Wearing a kilt as if it was a flag, poet and patriarch Hugh MacDiarmid wanted to erect cultural barbed wire between Scotland and England, whereas Alexander Trocchi, a novelist of the younger generation, was for a much more open give-and-take. The two extremists thundered at each other, watched and listened to by a bemused Mailer, who was soberly well dressed, with even his wild locks under control. He could have passed himself off as the U.S. Ambassador to the Court of St. James, a swinging Kennedy businessman. Was this the influence of M'lady?

At a session on commitment, the conference shot from local fears about losing one's roots to international concerns. A message was read from Alan Paton, author of *Cry, the Beloved Country*. He couldn't attend the conference because the South African government had deprived him of his passport. Paton's voice of commitment to Christian ideals in opposition to his government's stifling racial policies made all the other speeches sound comfortably, even complacently secure as the luckier writers pronounced their own commitments—to themselves or to love, to death, to truth, to communism, or to homosexuality, or to tolerance . . . Oh, to everything, apparently, if you added it all up. Paton summed up the past year in a grim line: "The freedom to write and publish took a great beating." Here was one white writer Baldwin would surely have identified with. Could Mailer's expression, as he listened, have been one of deep envy? Certainly when his time came to speak, he didn't try to rival Paton; not a word about the racial scene in his own country. He quickly returned to his own obsessions.

For Mailer, the Western writer was a Faustian who always entered into a contract outside of himself, whether it was with an ideal or a drug. Western man seemed bound to be committed to what Mailer called An Other. More writers spoke up—L.P. Hartley, Mary McCarthy again, Rebecca West, Richard Hughes—and Mailer retired modestly into the background. At least for the time being. You couldn't have asked for a more obliging visiting writer. Lady Jeanne would have been proud of him; as the British say, meaning it as a compliment, she could take him anywhere. Only those who had expected some temperamental explosion were disappointed, and most concluded that his reputation was unfair to him—to Nice Norman. As I watched him listening with apparent interest, however far away his mind was, smiling benignly, nodding modestly, he reminded me of a big-time politician giving his performance as a regular guy. He'd told me once, "We want our presidents above all to be likable—that's far more important than their being brilliant. We want them to be as available, as understandable, as pleasant, as the used-car salesman next door or the high school principal down the street." Were we watching Mailer the used-car salesman, Mailer the high school principal?

If so, he soon tired of the role. Next day he took part in a strange press conference with Henry Miller and Muriel Spark, an English satirical novelist who was just becoming well known, thanks to exposure in *The New Yorker*. Mailer and Miller claimed that a writer had a commitment to the under-

71

dog, the underprivileged, whereas Muriel Spark, looking like a flustered English housewife when her guests are getting tight, appealed for understanding for the overdog as well, which clearly made the other two impatient. "In every underdog there's an overdog attempting to come out," murmured Lawrence Durrell, but the argument petered out when Miss Spark admitted to a spiritual commitment—to Roman Catholicism— that Mailer and Miller seemed to think made any further discussion pointless.

Angus Wilson went back to a concrete example—how welcome it was in the chaos of generalizations!—and described a meeting with Alan Paton, that private man forced to make a public stand. He contrasted Paton's moral courage with the moral cowardice of some other white South Africans—"nullities," he called them—with whom he'd stayed on a visit to that country. Mailer appeared to listen closely; he was poker-faced.

But when a message was read out from Mikhail Sholokov, the novelist of Soviet heroes, regretting that he couldn't leave the Soviet Union to attend the conference because of "parliamentary duties," Mailer grinned in recognition of a familiar gambit for staying out of trouble. It was as if he might have blamed his own absence not on the arrival of his daughter but on running for mayor—for president. But there was this difference still: Sholokov was a solid establishment man, a Deputy of the Supreme Soviet, who never risked anything, whereas Mailer wasn't established at all and, at least until recently, had risked his life and his reputation; he was a long way off being able to merge writer and politician as completely as the Russian —and no doubt Mailer's truest admirers hoped he never would.

He was now visibly getting his confidence back, and he became playful. In a discussion on censorship, he impersonated a "civilized" censor who liked literature but feared too much sophisticated sex in books might weaken the war potential of the nation. Thus while seeming to be devil's advocate, Mailer slyly took a few cracks at the American Establishment, the warmongers, the police, the clergy, and the puritanical. He obviously had Mary McCarthy, who was presiding at the session, worried about whether to take his censorship fantasy seriously, especially when he cast a kind eye on such anticensorship works as those of Henry Miller, William Burroughs, and "the *early* Mary McCarthy." But no one needed to worry. He was affable and talked softly; Nice Norman was still with us. If a vote for the most popular had been taken at that moment, he would have been an easy winner.

News of his performance must have crossed the Atlantic and there were obviously some unbelievers who were still living in the past. A cable to the organizers arrived from a worried young New York poet: "Please confirm Norman really delegate at official writers' conference." Was the young poet worried about a potential betrayal, that yet another rebel might have gone over to the Establishment?

I remember seeing Mailer standing between Henry Miller and William Burroughs. For many in the audience, they were the prime rebels of the gathering, and yet what a contrast they made! Miller and Burroughs were both tall, thin men, Miller a mellow lover of life and Burroughs more ascetic and solemn, while Mailer between them was like Sancho Panza to their Don Quixote, smaller, broader, competitive, and clownish. A fan who crept up on them to eavesdrop complained later that they had been talking about their royalties.

Burroughs arose to attack pornography in advertising. He had a serious, unchanging expression, and I imagined him cracking his knuckles while waiting for the right word; nobody would have recognized him as the beatnik hero, the drug addict's laureate, the author of *Naked Lunch,* which still wasn't published in Britain. Mailer had risen to its defense when it was attacked in the U.S. Burroughs told me, "In America, writers can say just about anything they want. The criterion is, I believe—and it seems silly to me—that you prove the book has a serious purpose. Who's to say that?" He said the only critic he remembered who had got the point of his work was . . . no, he didn't say Mailer, but Mary McCarthy. "She said mine was a carnival world, a circus world. Mine are carni-characters, con-world short-change artists. I have extended that to interplanetary fields with interplanetary con men and gunmen, short-change artists who shortchange in terms of space instead of time. This has all come from the world I have had contact with, very much a part of the American scene, really, though by no means confined to America."

He complained now to the conference that censorship prevented much scientific research into sex by which perhaps it might be possible to determine precisely which sex practices were healthy and which harmful. Henry Miller appealed simply for "the good life" because he regarded the whole planet as "strangled."

The third rebel acted as a somewhat whimsical chairman of a session on the future of the novel—would that troubled young New York poet have recognized Mailer in the chair? Lawrence Durrell put his faith in electronic computers. He had visited one at Edinburgh University that could write sonnets; by Christmas it might have written its first novel. Part of the audience didn't know whether to laugh or cry. Mailer thought the novel's future lay in the relationship with the physical world. He considered *Das Kapital* a great novel, the first to have a commodity as its hero. For this reason he found the experimental French novelist Robbe-Grillet interesting if virtually unreadable. Some of the audience clearly didn't know if he was serious or not; his jocular manner didn't help. The future novel, he went on, offered a way of coming to terms with the material world, this plastic trap in which we had to live. The hero of the future novel would be the man who could tame the inventions of man.

Banned books displayed—but not for sale—at this censorship session, including two by de Sade, were withdrawn after a visit by police officers. It was denied the police visit had caused the books to be withdrawn, but in any case none of the writers discussing censorship seemed to want to get into it and find some occasion for heroics.

Mailer told me the best part of the conference for him was the opportunity it afforded him to spend some time with Henry Miller. Miller, too, had once gone to extremes and survived.

"He could have been an American heterosexual Genêt," Mailer said admiringly. But that wasn't enough. "He had enough talent to become an American Shakespeare." But that apparently wasn't enough, either. He wasn't afraid of the unpopular sewers of existence. Nor was he trapped in the ego. One felt that what Mailer most admired was that Miller wasn't running for anything; he would risk ruin for truth. He made both Mailer the politician and Mailer the romantic realize the shortcomings of ambition. Miller at that time was Mailer's ideal self.

7

Violence was escalating fast that year; Europe was like a calm backwater. The situation reached a weird climax when the U.S. Army had to occupy Oxford, Mississippi, to ensure the safety of the first black student at the local university—James Meredith.

It was William Faulkner's hometown, and although he had been dead for several months, the scene might have been written by him. Lynching was in the air; local rednecks were coming into town loaded with weapons, as if they were in a Western; little old ladies talked as violently as the old dames of the French Revolution. President Kennedy called on the people of Mississippi to "cease and desist" and angered the blacks and moderate whites who objected to being included with the racists causing all the trouble. Kennedy had in effect addressed one side as if it was both.

When I arrived at night, the small local airport resembled the front lines, with armed soldiers and military equipment everywhere; we might have been back in the Korean War. Several times on the way into town my cab was stopped at roadblocks and we were searched for weapons. Our white skins automatically made us suspect.

Returning to New York was like coming out of a nightmare; I had never appreciated the city more. Baldwin was away—it was hard to find him home now, he was usually on the road lecturing or somewhere abroad—so there was no chance of discussing it with him, though his viewpoint would have been the kind of challenge I needed to be sure I fully understood what was happening.

I saw Mailer briefly, but on this subject his viewpoint was less of a challenge; he was on the same side of the racial frontier as I was, but curiously far from the front line for such an involved person. I had recently been reading an essay of his on Jean Genêt's play, *The Blacks,* in which he said that the Jews and the Negroes were two of the greatest peoples in America, but half of their populations had "sold themselves to the suburb, the center, the secure; that diarrhea of the spirit which is embodied in the fleshless query: 'Is this good for the Jews?' So went the Jew. So went the Negro. The mediocre among them rushed for the disease . . ."

When I talked with Mailer about the essay, he compared the Negroes' three centuries in America to the twenty centuries the Jews had wandered outside—he seemed to be presenting himself now much more as a Jew. He was even writing for *Commentary,* the Jewish intellectual magazine, which introduced him as a Jewish writer and intellectual who stood "outside the organized Jewish community." At least he was willing to stand up and be counted. He began an informal bimonthly column on Martin Buber's *Tales of the Hassidim* for *Commentary,* which seemed to me as impenetrable for a non-Jew as St. Thomas Aquinas's writings for a non-Catholic.

In *The Blacks* essay, he dismissed many of the Negro leaders for being "as colorless as our white leaders and all too many of the Negroes one knows have a dull militancy compared to the curve and art of personality their counterparts had even ten years ago." Maybe—or maybe it was the effect of Mailer's being ten years older himself, nostalgic for the "curve and art" of younger days. I could imagine how this might strike Baldwin as being in the same key as the myth of Negro sexuality and thus would enrage him. Could these two never agree now?

It certainly enraged Lorraine Hansberry, the straight-talking author of *A Raisin in the Sun,* the recent play about a black family's problems, which had astonished everyone by being a Broadway success. She called Mailer one of the "new paternalists." Mailer replied that they had a fundamental disagreement; whereas he believed there were qualities, essences, innate differences of being between white and black, she thought the only difference was pigmentation of the skin, that all else was environment. He challenged her and Baldwin to a three-cornered debate in Carnegie Hall. He also proposed that a touring company take *The Blacks* into the racist strongholds of the South with a white and black cast, and with some tough Village cats as bodyguards. I could imagine this melodramatic suggestion would seem mere playacting to Lorraine Hansberry and Baldwin—the kind of playacting a white could do over a racial matter because he wasn't on the receiving end and therefore not deeply concerned. I was sure Mailer's cavalier attitude covered up a deep seriousness, but it was a luxury in the circumstances. His touch in racial matters was strangely uneasy, unsure, almost embarrassed.

Mailer ran into Baldwin a few nights later in the White Horse Tavern, famous as a gathering place for Village artists and intellectuals. Baldwin was furious, Mailer said. "You're not responsible," Baldwin told Mailer. It was easy to picture Baldwin's eyes widening fiercely and his finger wagging as Mailer tensed like a boxer. "We had another brotherly quarrel," Mailer summed up. "Brotherly" at least was a concession, as long as he didn't mean Cain and Abel.

"He still sees us as goddam romantic black symbols," Baldwin told me. "We still haven't been granted ordinary human status, the right to go to the bathroom. Until Norman sees us with no more romanticism than he views Jewish storekeepers, he'll never understand or be on to what's happening, *really* happening."

The more successful they became, the more they seemed to be growing apart.

On magazine assignments, they both covered a world heavyweight boxing match between Floyd Patterson and Sonny Liston. Patterson and Liston were both black, but the resemblance stopped there. Although Patterson had been wild in his youth, he had reformed and was now regarded as an exemplary citizen. Nobody could say that of Liston. He had a criminal history and still talked rough and tough, though when he relaxed he had an engaging honesty. Their fight was soon regarded as a racial battle between Conformist and Outlaw, or Good and Evil; Patterson was so strongly supported by whites that there was some danger of his being considered an Uncle Tom by young streetwise blacks.

Mailer had recently been growing not only more publicly Jewish but also more Hemingwayish, and he had moved into boxing and tried to take over the big fights the way Papa had; Patterson and Liston were going to be looked over by Papa Mailer as plain fighters—none of that racial shit. Baldwin, however, had none of Mailer's devotion to the fight game; he was as uneasy in a gym as he was on a beach; he had no interest in athletics, in sports, in that kind of competition. His interest in Patterson and Liston was in their blackness, in their common experience; he wanted Patterson to win, but the fight itself probably appalled him deep down—the prospect of black boys, brothers, knocking hell out of each other for the amusement and profit of whites.

Baldwin's magazine story showed his uneasiness, his lack of interest; it wasn't written with the usual verve and confidence; and he has never republished it in his subsequent collections, nor has he covered any more big fights. Mailer's piece showed the difference between them. He was in a scene that suited the role he wanted to play. Here he was a male warrior among warriors, a White Negro assessing, dissecting his black brothers. He began by brooding over his role—that of a reporter; such casting was acceptable as long as it was on his terms. Yet his mere acceptance marked a change, a limit he had now given to his experience. Gone were the days of trying to make the action, of dominating it, creating it, at extremes of experience; perhaps they were gone forever. Now he would report the activities of others, provided he could also be a part of their action—not a star part but a vivid supporting role. More than

79

most writers, he was impatient with a sedentary typewriter role; he wanted that, but also much more—how much, however, was he willing to risk for it now? Being a reporter was as far as you could go unless you were willing to risk everything, and a part of him no doubt cautioned him: Never again. So here he was reporting the Patterson-Liston experience, yet trying to find a way into it for himself; he was trying to turn the so-called objective reality of the reporter into Moravia's subjective reality.

He touched on everything from homosexuality again ("The accusation of homosexuality arouses a major passion in many men; they spend their lives resisting it with a biological force. . . .") to why Negroes preferred Patterson to Liston ("Now as the Negro was beginning to come into the white man's world, he wanted the logic of the white man's world: annuities, mental hygiene, sociological jargon, committee solutions for the ills of the breast. He was sick of a whore's logic and a pimp's logic, he wanted no more of *mother-wit,* of *smarts,* or *playing the dozens,* of battling for true love into the diamond-hard eyes of every classy prostitute and hustler on the street. The Negro wanted Patterson, because Floyd was the proof a man could be successful and yet be secure. If Liston won, the old torment was open again. . . .") There were brilliant perceptions, but there was also a tendency to put The Negro into a tight intellectual pigeonhole that Mailer would probably have rejected for people he knew better; there was also a sense of showing off, with those references to *smarts* and *playing the dozens.* My God, our boy knows his way around; here's one cracker who's been there.

Neither Mailer nor Baldwin turned out to be good judges, for Liston easily demolished their man Patterson. Mailer, however, was a bad loser. He announced that he knew a way Patterson could win the rematch. It sounded unlikely. Patterson, who was really not heavy enough to be a heavyweight, had been demolished so quickly that Baldwin had come up with a startled, "What happened?" There was no indication that Patterson could do any better next time (and of course he didn't), but Mailer thought otherwise; his competitive sense, the urge to share the spotlight, drove him to challenge the winner himself. He tried to take over Liston's post-fight press conference. More artful than he was ever given credit for, Liston put down Mailer as smartly as he had dealt with Patterson. He called Mailer a "bum," later softening it by saying we were all bums, and he suggested Mailer had been drinking. Maybe he had been. His enemies dismissed his performance as an attempt to share Liston's spotlight. But there was more to it than that; Mailer was creating a situation in which he could learn more about his complex subject—Liston; once more understanding was supposed to come out of conflict. Mailer himself was as ever touchingly repentant. Yet again, he told himself, he'd tried to become a hero and had ended instead as an eccentric.

Mailer and Baldwin had sat at the ringside one seat apart. They were becoming for some people the literary equivalent of Patterson and Liston, and this meeting with an empty seat separating them looked symbolic. When would their big fight take place? Mailer admitted there had been "a chill" between them for the last year—"not a feud, but bad feeling." Although they tried to be friendly at the ringside, the "unsettled differences" were still there. They had a small fight at a party, though it didn't come to blows; the combinations were all wordy. "We each insulted the other's good intentions," Mailer reported, "and turned away." At the end of the fight, both having bet on Patterson, they attempted to bury their quarrel in mutual disappointment—or so Mailer hoped. "This time it might stay buried for a while."

Baldwin said, "My Lord, I lost seven hundred and fifty dollars tonight." That was a long way from Horatio Street days and changing checks in bars. Mailer commented: "Well, we laughed." The laugh anyway was really his. "I had lost no more than a paltry twenty-eight." They went off their own ways to fight another day.

With Mailer, personal relations, politics, almost anything seemed to be discussed now in the language of boxing, much as Hemingway used to talk. Mailer had had a debate with right-winger William F. Buckley, Jr., who was nearly as good as

Mailer at promoting himself, and Mailer said of this easygoing confrontation between two white polemicists: "I had felt exactly like a club fighter who has won a very big fight." Was he rehearsing for Baldwin? Baldwin also took on Buckley—in England—and the result, with an audience almost wholly on Baldwin's side, must have indicated to Mailer that the time was not ready yet for their big fight; he didn't want to play Patterson to Baldwin's Liston. Anyway both of them seemed to debate anybody and everybody except each other. Success perhaps had made them both more cautious; success and the years. Mailer had justified himself—the change in him—in *The Deer Park:* "There was that law of life, so cruel and so just, which demanded that one must grow or else pay more for remaining the same."

When I saw Baldwin next for a drink and a talk, he told me about a long essay he'd written for *The New Yorker* magazine; he thought it summed up his thinking and experience and would greatly enlarge his audience. Part of it, he said, involved his meeting with the Black Muslims, the most militant and separatist of the black religious organizations. Baldwin had met the Honorable Elijah Muhammad, the leader of the Nation of Islam, the Black Muslims' formal title.

"I told him I'd left the church twenty years ago and I haven't joined anything since. It was my way of telling him I didn't intend to join the Muslims and become James X." Elijah Muhammad had patiently inquired what he was now. Baldwin had replied: "Nothing. I'm a writer. I like doing things alone." He also said defiantly that he had some white friends and he didn't care if whites and blacks married. Elijah replied that Baldwin *might* have white friends, or think he did, and they *might* be trying to be decent—now—but that their time was up. Baldwin told me: "I knew two or three white people I'd trust with my life. Others I knew were struggling to do their best, to make the world more human. But I couldn't convey this to him. He just looked at me with pity. All my examples were merely exceptions." Baldwin said he was calling his essay *The Fire Next Time.*

Elijah and the Muslims made Baldwin seem almost a moderate, an integrationist; I tried to imagine Mailer taking them on —Mailer versus the Muslims—instead of William Buckley, much as he had confronted Liston. Elijah would have been equally good at the put-down, though "bum" wouldn't have been his word; maybe "devil." Mailer, the White Negro, would have become a White Devil; it was a title that might have appealed to him. Would Baldwin have played the exorcist? Baldwin seemed to be somewhere between Elijah and Mailer, though it was obvious which of the two he would lean toward . . . it wouldn't be Mailer.

Baldwin's novel, *Another Country*, had been published just before *The Fire Next Time;* it, too, dealt with relations between blacks and whites, and it had a much greater success than anyone expected. It began with a quotation from Henry James ("They strike one, above all, as giving no account of themselves in any terms already consecrated by human use . . .") I said I hadn't expected to find him quoting James; temperamentally they seemed so different. "He's one of my favorite writers," Baldwin told me. "A relative of his gave me a signed picture of him. I hang it over my work table."

I said I thought imitators of Henry James today—several novelists received excellent reviews for writing imitation James —made the mistake of choosing similar subjects to those of James's novels. If James were alive today and living in the U.S., he surely wouldn't write about the class divisions and relationships. What would fascinate him would be the line where whites and blacks met; to a contemporary James, race would be what class had been to the real James.

"It would be hard for such a fastidious man to get enough experience," Baldwin said. His eyes widened as he thought about it. "Yet, you know, he was so perceptive that a single incident or person might give him a whole scene. People make the mistake of thinking him snobbish. Snobbery is a form of blindness. James wasn't blind; he could see *through* things."

I told him how much I admired the character of Rufus in *Another Country,* and Baldwin was obviously pleased. "I knew someone who died like that—a friend of mine." I asked him if the bar and grill on 42nd Street that Rufus went in was Grant's, a legendary meeting place between Seventh and Eighth avenues, since closed and replaced by Kentucky Fried Chicken. Baldwin nodded, his mind still on Henry James, as he showed a moment later when he said: "We are all victims of our environment. James grew up a certain way and he had only that to write about. I'm the same, Mailer's the same, all of us. We have to accept our restrictions. What's important is what we make of them. Henry James did wonders with his."

Baldwin hesitated, as if slightly embarrassed. "I'm talking like a writer again. It seems so long since I have. I'm almost invariably asked about racial matters now. I feel like a politician, not a writer, and it's not a good feeling. I have no wish to run for anything."

"Unlike Mailer. He still seems to want to be mayor."

"God knows why. Well, Norman can have it as far as I'm concerned."

I had been reading some André Gide and I remembered Baldwin's essay, "The Male Prison." Baldwin said he disliked Gide for his Protestantism and his homosexuality; he had not come to terms with either. "His work is so cold, so wintry, it verges on the inhuman. I can't care for his people at all. I don't know what repressed him the more, his religion or his nature. Protestantism isn't right any more than any other religion, but it can be right for you; so it's not a matter of asking whether you agree with it but whether it helps your life. Similarly it's not a matter of whether homosexuality is right, but whether you can deal with it, whether it's a part of the natural, human you. Nothing is natural if it makes you inhuman."

The Fire Next Time was published in The New Yorker and created a sensation; it wasn't that it said anything Baldwin hadn't said before, but it brought it all together for a new, influential audience. Time magazine said the 20,000-word essay showed Baldwin "as the most bitterly eloquent voice of the American Negro. Yet it also shows him as one who speaks less for the Negro than to the white—and it is in that sense that he is most compelling." The same issue of *Time* selected Pope John as Man of the Year ("To the world at large, John has given what neither science nor diplomacy can provide: a sense of its unity as the human family. . . ."). *The Fire Next Time,* which conveyed a similar sense of human unity and the price for disregarding it, came out as a book and was soon on the best-seller list.

I was in London shortly afterward and received a phone call from Baldwin who was passing through on the way to somewhere else—I forget where, probably Paris or Turkey, his two European favorites at that time. That familiar intense voice told me to lose no time in coming over to his hotel. When I got there, a fifth of Johnny Walker was already open and Baldwin was being interviewed by Donald Hinds, a local correspondent for a West Indian newspaper. Although he was now used to being interviewed, Baldwin responded freshly to the questions and also asked some questions back about the treatment of West Indians in England. The answers he received were depressing; he didn't escape by leaving home.

He was accompanied by a friend, a young painter from Brooklyn. While Baldwin went off to visit his English publisher, I took the young painter to see some of the sights of London and he sent off picture postcards to his family in Brooklyn and to his local minister. Baldwin obviously saw him as his young self and was trying to give him the same experience of Europe he had had, but without the grim struggle for existence.

Baldwin came back with a young Indian—not American Indian—who worked for his publisher, and during the kind of noisy arguments that are produced by mixing together Americans, Europeans, and Asians, spurred on by heavy doses of Johnny Walker Red, Baldwin volunteered to show the Indian and the English what they had been missing all these years— soul food. We all moved on to the young Indian's apartment, and while Baldwin took over the kitchen, the rest of us sat around talking and drinking like a bunch of students. "Remember, I helped my mother bring up a large family," Baldwin told

85

us midway through his preparations as if allaying fears of what was to come out of the kitchen. "What I don't know about cooking, baby, ain't worth knowing." I began to wonder if he was trying to boost his own confidence; those days of helping to bring up the family were far behind him, and I had had some bad experiences with amateur cooks. But what finally emerged on the table justified all his boasting—and he even volunteered to do all the washing up afterward.

Next day, in return for the banquet of soul food—while the young painter went off to select some presents to take home to Brooklyn—I bought Baldwin a slap-up lunch in an olde worlde restaurant off Baker Street. An ancient waiter served us with grave courtesy; for some reason I didn't quite understand, this moved Baldwin deeply. He said the service seemed to treat him like an equal human being; for once a waiter was not making him feel like a nigger. I still didn't quite get it—surely he had been in many restaurants where the waiters had been similarly professional and polite. Perhaps it was his mood that day; perhaps it was because Baker Street brought back memories. "I came over once with . . . oh, I suppose you'd call them hustlers, maybe even gangsters. I was dependent on them. I had nothing. Now . . ." Now his luck had certainly changed and perhaps that was what made his mood so responsive and grateful. He insisted on adding to the adequate tip I'd left the old waiter. "I'll remember this day . . ."

When we got back to Baldwin's hotel, the young painter had already returned, loaded with his gifts. Baldwin told him he had decided to give him a trip to Greece so he could do some painting there before he returned to Brooklyn; he'd be able to pick up some more gifts for the family in Athens or some other part of Greece. A Mediterranean adventure sounded like a fine idea, but when he learned that Baldwin wouldn't be going with him, the young painter wasn't keen to make the trip. The prospect of being alone in a foreign country obviously scared him. Baldwin pooh-poohed his fears. You had to take opportunities when they were offered, he said, because they seldom came a second time. You also had to do things on your own, for then you learned to be independent. "If it's easy, don't do it," Baldwin said. He tried to draw me in as an ally, but I kept out of it. I was sympathetic to the young painter—he was far from Brooklyn and I knew how he must feel, even in England, where at least he could make himself understood. He was at the stage Baldwin had been at when he first went to Paris. Baldwin had made himself sternly independent, had become a self-reliant cosmopolitan, but the process had taken years. The young painter had probably seen enough for one trip. I left them arguing about it.

8

The restlessness that seemed to be everywhere—was there ever a period when change was so much in the air?—showed up in my own life and I changed jobs and also continents. From being a wandering reporter in Europe with occasional assignments in America, I joined *Newsweek* magazine as a writer in New York.

The journalists on *Newsweek* were the same as journalists everywhere—bright, frustrated men and women who could tell only half of what they knew (the other half was often reserved for some great—but as yet unwritten—novel), experienced in watching the famous and powerful, but often woefully ignorant of other ways of life. American journalism in those days was still almost totally white, and reporters became experts overnight in the racial field because they had once interviewed Malcolm X or covered a riot.

For a reporter like me, whose faith was based on seeing for himself, like the disciple Thomas, this lack of direct experience explained a lot of the decisions and news values about the black and white confrontations. It also made the work hard for me. I had learned to distrust any eyes or ears except my own, and now I had to accustom myself to writing stories based on what someone else in some faraway bureau of the magazine had seen.

Baldwin at that time was very much in the headlines and I thought possibly the magazine could make use of my knowledge of him. After I had established myself in the National

Affairs section with several stories, I suggested to an executive editor that *Newsweek* do a cover story on Baldwin. He was a brisk, unstuffy, enthusiastic man, the kind of shirt-sleeves journalist I enjoyed working with, and he took suggestions seriously even when he didn't agree with them. He called me into his office and talked for a long time, explaining why he didn't feel that Baldwin was important enough for a cover story—cover stories were regarded as the equivalent of knighthoods in England. Baldwin seemed to make him strangely uneasy and I couldn't tell why; he didn't explain; it was simply in his attitude, his manner. It couldn't have been Baldwin's blackness, because he didn't have the same attitude toward Martin Luther King; it reminded me of some people's attitude toward Mailer after the stabbing incident—as if he challenged their values, their way of life, too much, and they had to put down either him or themselves.

The executive's attitude also reminded me of some of Mailer's early cracks about Baldwin, the perfume-fuck-you nonsense. Baldwin didn't meet their male chauvinist standards; their values, reflected in their sports and their politics and their journalism and so on, meant nothing to him; he even condemned them. So boosting Baldwin in a way would be like boosting an enemy of all you lived by.

A modest man when it came to Culture—his great interest was in action stories, so-called hard news—the *Newsweek* executive backed up his opinion by quoting a professor of English he knew as a fellow commuter. The professor had told him that Baldwin wasn't an important writer. I frankly thought this was ridiculous, and to try to make the point effectively, I told him a story about Robert Frost. In his famous poem "Stopping by Woods on a Snowy Evening," Frost's horse gave his harness bells a shake to ask if there was some mistake in stopping in the middle of nowhere. Frost told me with a mischievous look that a doubting professor had asked the famous Texan horseman, Frank Dobie, if a horse could ask a question, and Frost approvingly quoted Dobie's reply: "A horse can ask better questions than most professors."

89

The anecdote had no effect on the *Newsweek* executive, however, and so I gave up. I wasn't one of those on-the-road reporters who enjoyed baiting academics, but I thought this reverence for the professor's opinion of Baldwin reflected a growing tendency in journalism to accept academic specialists at face value, perhaps because, unlike the previous generation, most journalists now passed through college before entering the profession.

Shortly after I made my suggestion at *Newsweek, Time* devoted a cover story to Baldwin. There was an intense, brotherly rivalry between the two newsmagazines over their cover stories; many of their writers had worked on both magazines and did a lot of socializing together, but they always tried to keep close-mouthed about their cover subjects until the magazine was published. *Time*'s appearance with Baldwin certainly legitimized my idea and belittled the professor's assessment, and, in fact, the day it appeared on the newsstands, I was called into the executive's room again. "Looks like I made a mistake," he said ruefully.

Time put its story in its national affairs section, not among its books. Baldwin had made it not as a mere writer, but as an activist, a spokesman. Mailer, I thought, would probably be green with envy. He, who had been famous first, was being left behind!

With a photograph showing Baldwin—in a suit!—addressing students at the University of California, *Time* described him as "a nervous, slight, almost fragile figure, filled with frets and fears. He is effeminate in manner, drinks considerably, smokes cigarettes in chains, and he often loses his audience with overblown arguments. Nevertheless, in the U.S. today there is not another writer, white or black, who expresses with such poignancy and abrasiveness the dark realities of the racial ferment in North and South."

The same issue of the magazine also had a lead story about the racial conflict in Birmingham, Alabama, the symbol of segregation, which Martin Luther King was assaulting in his determined nonviolent way. *Time* described King as "the

Negroes' inspirational but sometimes inept leader." I wondered if the *Time* writer, in saying that, knew what the "sometimes inept" King was up against. *Time*'s story and its statistics—eighteen racial bombings, so many that Negroes called the city Bombingham, and fifty cross burnings in the previous six years—didn't convey the extent of segregation. Schools, restaurants, drinking fountains, toilets were all still segregated, and Public Safety Commissioner Eugene (Bull) Connor headed an army of club-swinging cops to make sure they remained so. King told me once, a temporarily depressed King, that he felt as if he was trying to cut his way through a brick wall with his finger-nails. . . .

When next I saw Baldwin, I congratulated him on his *Time* cover—he shrugged it off—and I asked him about his experiences in hopping from city to city to talk to college and high school students, a schedule of speaking engagements a presidential candidate could hardly have beaten. While we were talking, a lieutenant from one of the civil rights organizations came with a draft of some statement and they retired into Baldwin's study for Baldwin to revise it. I saw his photograph of Henry James above the desk; I wondered if he sometimes yearned in the heat of battle to get back to the privacy of authorship.

I noticed a slight change in him when he argued. He would occasionally use a collective "I" in the dramatic style of a preacher; for example, with finger wagging, his voice rising, he would tell some obstinate white: "I dammed a lot of rivers, I laid a lot of track, I hoed a lot of cotton, I cleaned a lot of dishes. You wouldn't have had this country if it hadn't been for me . . ."

I noticed a rising impatience in him and, with the stories of brutality against Negroes filling the newspapers and magazines, who could blame him?

I was there one night when a white friend of his brought along a couple of his white friends. They seemed to be a middle-class pair of unremarkable complacency; not Baldwin's kind of people, I would have said, but I had seen him easily accept

91

similar couples when they came with other friends. This particular time, though, something about them irritated him, or perhaps they became simply the target of a general anger and frustration. Whatever the reason, Baldwin started to attack their few remarks about what was happening in the country; he became a collective black "I" while they suddenly became a collective white "You," responsible for all the sins of the whites; Bull Connor was their brother, their responsibility. The couple tried feebly to reply, to accept no responsibility, but Baldwin wouldn't let them escape so easily. He kept leveling accusations at them—what had they done about this injustice, that one, the other one, all the injustices "You" had caused? The woman gave up first, rather tearfully; the man then did a machismo act in defense of her. But Baldwin's anger was unappeasable; his finger went on wagging, his eyes widened accusingly, his voice rose, and he prosecuted and judged the couple guilty—the now silent, red-faced couple, bewildered by what was happening.

I understood that Baldwin was releasing an enormous tension the way soldiers will go on the town and smash glasses and fight with bouncers. What I couldn't understand was why the fellow who had brought the couple remained silent and watched his two friends attacked and condemned. Loyalty surely demanded that he rise to their defense and try to divert Baldwin's wrath, but instead he watched them be shot down and finally run for their lives without intervening. I couldn't believe that Baldwin liked his silence—his betrayal. In Baldwin's present mood, it probably summed up for him how undependable whites were as allies; he was near to that Muslim mood he had criticized in *The Fire Next Time*.

The anger slowly receded and he sat back, Scotch in hand, brooding. Nobody broke the silence. His friend watched him, not knowing what to say, unwilling to risk being the target of another eruption.

"Have another drink, Jimmy," I said at last.

His big eyes contemplated me, coldly at first, and then suddenly his whole face lit up: the storm had passed. He said quietly: "I guess I did overdo it." But he obviously didn't want that interpreted as meaning he regretted all he had said to the now departed couple.

He said, his voice rising emotionally: "It's ignorance like that that has made the whole situation in this country possible. They are too innocent, too well-meaning"—he seemed to spit out the words—"to live. Northern whites like them haven't even learned to *see* us. And the problem for Southern whites is that they see us all the time. We are therefore ignored in the North and under surveillance in the South—a kind of ward or a victim. Both must change before either will."

He refilled his glass; he seldom ate; it was Scotch that was keeping him going. "Real men, not the white imitations, accept each other, trust, celebrate what's constant in life, and are ready for what must change. Change means renewal. But life itself becomes impossible if you refuse to accept change. There is simply no renewal possible, and without renewal, in time there will be no life. White people, being in a phony privileged position at our expense, don't want change; they feel they have too much to lose. They have! Bobby Kennedy assures us that a Negro can become president in forty years, but he means that will be possible if the Negro first of all accepts and adopts white standards. A White Negro can become president in forty years! That isn't acceptance, it isn't justice, it isn't anything but the same old game . . ."

It was the first time I'd heard him use Bobby Kennedy as a put-down example. He had seemed at one time to flirt with the Kennedys the way Mailer had done. I remembered his slightly breathless reference to the White House at the time of the Prix Formentor. He was more used to the trappings, the pressures, of fame now; nobody could con him, certainly not the Kennedys. If this was the best the Democrats, the white liberals, could do, then it was his duty to point out how far short they still were from what was needed. He was free to criticize, to challenge the Kennedys in a way Mailer could never be.

Mailer had written a long piece helping Kennedy to get elected; at one time Mailer had seen himself as the kingmaker.

He had romantic hopes, real commitments he couldn't give up; the more Kennedy disappointed him, the worse the alternatives —Nixon and Co.—seemed. Mailer agonized over Jack's unconventional personality and his conventional politics; to appreciate Mailer's inhibitions in Baldwin's terms, you had to look at Baldwin's position over Martin Luther King.

For Baldwin, King's familiar Biblical style was something he'd left behind when he gave up religion as a boy preacher. And then there was King's black middle-class background, to which a poor Harlem boy was bound to feel unsympathetic, if not downright antagonistic. But beyond all that—on the credit side—Martin was black and risking his life; any criticism from Baldwin had to be muted or it would seem tantamount to a betrayal of a brother—a Judas act. Mailer couldn't feel as strongly about Kennedy—white didn't identify with white the same way as black identified with black—but there was enough in common, enough of a commitment, enough romantic hope riding on Kennedy, for Mailer to feel inhibited in criticizing him. He could be no more free with Kennedy than Baldwin was with King. The racial loyalties were still pretty rigid when it got to the level of the unconscious, the instinct; there was still a grave problem of identification across racial lines—white might "understand"; so might black. But identify? Hardly ever.

The March on Washington, the huge procession of witness by blacks and whites, which reached its climax with King's "I Have a Dream" speech, had so scared the Kennedy administration that they tried to stop it. If it had been a vast white gathering, it was a fair bet the president would have addressed it; but because it was a predominantly black occasion for a black cause, *the* black cause, Kennedy received the leaders behind the scenes. There were too many white middle-class votes to be lost by identifying the presidency with the black cause; it was still a case of "they" shall overcome, not "we." The times needed a leader who would be willing to risk rejection or defeat, but you might as well tell a swimmer to go drown himself as urge a politician to endanger his chances of re-election. Kennedy would only go so far; he would attempt to outmaneuver the devils of prejudice rather than corner and confront them.

No wonder Baldwin was impatient, critical, challenging. Mailer needed all his intellectual skills to find rationalizations to justify his loyalty; his White Negroes who had been for Kennedy now grew restless, disillusioned. He might soon be in danger of losing them, like the troubled young poet who had cabled the Edinburgh Festival. At this rate, when he did run for mayor, he might already have lost the majority of his supporters from the old days without gaining enough new replacements. How long would his loyalty to Kennedy stand the strain?

Bobby Kennedy—often the troubleshooter, or advance patrol, for his brother—translated the administration's fear of where the civil rights movement was heading into a series of talks with what he regarded as key people. He wanted answers to basic questions: whom the Negroes listened to—and who spoke for them. The old Red paranoia was there, too: were the Communists infiltrating the movement? Was there any risk that the nation's enemies could make use of the situation? Kennedy pursued the answers with energy and zeal. His simplifications were almost touching in their essential innocence; he had a politician's craving for easy solutions, a college boy's faith in power through education.

Baldwin might be appalled by his ignorance—did the president, too, know so little about blacks?—and yet RFK's eagerness to find out made him seem healthy, liberal and committed, compared with most politicians, who kept pace with the most conservative voters. Bobby at least wanted to learn, to go out ahead. Mailer would give him good marks for that, perhaps would even admire his willingness to risk a put-down from some black cats. Baldwin, however, was not willing to concede him that much; he told me he was "chilled" by the expression in Bobby Kennedy's eyes.

I knew what he meant. When I met Kennedy, his whole manner was so repressed that he seemed in danger of bursting open at any moment; it was as though his personality had been too tightly corseted. It was apparently impossible for him to relax, to be open. And he approached other people as if they should be the same, submitting their problems to the techniques he had learned as an undergraduate, reducing life to a tidy seminar. I wondered what he expected when he asked Jimmy Baldwin—he had a football coach's belief in first-name terms—to introduce him to some people, to bring along a group of Negro spokesmen. He no doubt felt that he was taming firebrand Baldwin and making use of him; it was an ego trip to go into the lions' den and rap with one of the lions. Bobby could have foreseen no risk, for everyone was impressed by the Kennedy name and the power of the White House; surely Baldwin could be expected to bring along a tame group for a respectful exchange.

What transpired was something else. Baldwin took with him the kind of group that might have been sitting around his apartment when the call came. Harry Belafonte, the singer; Lena Horne, another singer; Baldwin's brother, David; Lorraine Hansberry; Jerome Smith, a young Freedom Rider, who had been badly beaten down South; Dr. Kenneth Clarke, the black expert in education; Baldwin's literary agent; several white show business people. . . . The group had none of the neatness or the meekness Kennedy was used to and probably expected.

I have heard several versions of what went on, including Baldwin's, and read other accounts. They all differ (hardly anyone can give an accurate report of an event even immediately afterward), but at least all the versions, accounts, reports and gossip agree that the early politeness, even friendliness, changed to open hostility before the end.

Bobby Kennedy apparently began by trotting out a few earnest clichés; the administration was deeply concerned and wanted fresh ideas on what to do. He seemed oblivious of the deep resentment against the administration's failure to take a strong stand; pragmatism all along the line—liberal here, conservative there—even some bad racist appointments to pay off some election-year debts. It was merely a political problem for Bobby; his experience of the black scene was that of a safe voyeur, and it was not enough to shake him out of the mold he was set in. He was a voyeur, too, at this meeting, which he intended to guide along the familiar lines that suited him. But he didn't allow for the deep personal involvement of many of the people there—the intense identification with the blacks who were being beaten and jailed down South while Bobby educated himself.

Soon this deep-freeze intellectual attitude of Kennedy's was too much for Jerome Smith, a large, mild young man who spoke with the authority of his wounds. "It makes me nauseous to be here," he apparently said at last.

Imagine Bobby's anger! Here he had gone out of his way like no other politician—white politician—to get a sounding. He, the crown prince of the Kennedys, had descended into the streets, and this was the way he was treated—by a mere kid who was as emotional as a woman! Tight-lipped, as authoritative and condescending as a high school principal interrupted by a student, Bobby is said to have snapped back: "I'm not going to sit here and listen to that kind of talk." It attacked not only his own sense of self-importance, his training in the cool, painless acquiring of experience, but also his loyalty to his brother—John Kennedy's administration was above reproach.

But Jerome Smith, the only person there from the front line, had many admirers in the room and Bobby wasn't allowed to put him down and take over. Impulsive, articulate Lorraine Hansberry told Bobby to think again, to examine his impatience. Having put down Mailer over *The Blacks,* she was quite ready to take on Bobby; both of them were among the "new paternalists."

Kennedy must have felt a little like the lord of the manor the day the servants rebelled. Or like a general meeting an enemy who breaks all the rules he has lived by; better to play chess with someone who kicks over the board. These people clearly felt no gratitude for his invitation, no sense of flattery at being singled out in the American game of winners and losers, the game he had been brought up on. He was told bluntly that they didn't see themselves as "exceptional Negroes," nor were they remotely interested in tea at the White House—a crack at the administration's use of social invitations to woo people (shades of Baldwin's lateness at Formentor! Would he accept an invitation now?).

The group tried to make it clear to Bobby that they felt one with the Negroes down South, and it was time the administration felt the same and acted accordingly. Bobby behaved as if he was shocked, Lorraine Hansberry told me later. He and his brother—he often talked as if that was the whole administration—were doing a good liberal job; couldn't these people see that? Didn't they feel at all *grateful?* He said later that the meeting was all emotion—as if emotion was a dirty word (perhaps, to such a repressed man, it was)—all *hysteria.* He showed no appreciation of the difference in styles between the involved and outsiders like himself; in the game of winners and losers, you are either right or wrong, for being right was the same as winning.

Bobby said he couldn't talk to the group as he could talk to blacks like Roy Wilkins of the National Association for the Advancement of Colored People (NAACP) or Martin Luther King. As two public figures who were in the political arena, they were willing to talk Kennedy's language, probably because they accepted his limitations of experience and had no real hope of a change in him. They weren't trying to educate him, but were merely trying to get something out of him—a little more positive action. They operated on the level of diplomacy, of negotiation; they couldn't afford to take Baldwin's risk, for they had something to lose, a whole army of supporters, a policy for change like a plan of battle, whereas Baldwin operated as an individual with nothing to lose but himself . . . and his family. Many a wealthier man, with a much more secure background to fall back on, wouldn't have risked making an enemy of ruthless Bobby, who was said to have ruined so many of his enemies.

Baldwin had had a sincere hope of changing Kennedy; in

that sense, he respected him more than people like King and Wilkins did; and for that reason, he felt let down afterward; he told me despairingly that Kennedy was deep down insensitive to the Negroes' torment.

Details of the meeting and its failure leaked out to the newspapers, and Baldwin became even more of a public personality. In American life, there seem to be two stages of fame; you first of all become famous for what you do and then you reach the point, God knows how or why or when, when what you do becomes almost irrelevant, and you are simply a celebrity. Baldwin seemed now to be reaching that second stage. His writing had been thrust into the background as the media concentrated on his activism; now his activism, his blackness, were becoming secondary to his public status: he had become a star of the gossip columns. It was possible to read the reports of the meeting with Kennedy without being aware that Baldwin was a writer.

When I first heard about the meeting, I failed to understand why Baldwin had taken along some of the people, especially a white actor and Baldwin's white man Friday at the time. Bobby Kennedy surely could be justifiably annoyed at receiving such people as spokesmen for the Negro. But when I thought about it more thoroughly, I appreciated better what Baldwin had been trying to do. He hadn't been conducting a seminar for Bobby Kennedy's instruction. He had tried instead to give him an actual experience—the kind of mixed, emotional rap session that was close to the heart of the civil rights movement and the black experience—that might help Kennedy far more to understand what was going on in the hearts of blacks than a few cool, reasoned speeches. Baldwin in effect had tried to take Kennedy's power and his money away from him and make him an equal in a rap in the living room, the kind of white-black confrontation that whites so seldom had.

I wondered how Mailer would have dealt with a similar situation; surely he would have approved of Baldwin's attempt to turn a routine meeting into an existential event (much as he had done himself with Sonny Liston's press conference), but

99

Mailer's style and selection would have been different. The old Harvard man might even have made a real seminar of it, with himself making a brilliant summary at the end. Certainly it would have been less haphazard, more planned and, I suspect, more to Kennedy's taste. If Mailer resisted his rebel's urge to dump a black prostitute in Bobby's lap, then he would have played the game Bobby knew, hoping for some kind of victory while playing within the rules. In this, he would have been as much a politician as Roy Wilkins or Martin Luther King; like them, he would have been willing to give a little in the hope of gaining a lot.

Lorraine Hansberry, that direct, honest lady, had once warned Mailer not to take the A train to Harlem if all he was going to meet were prostitutes and then generalize from them; a fraction of one per cent, she told him, couldn't represent the whole. It was she who had regretted that he hadn't called his White Negro essay something more modest, with no Negro connection, such as The Hipster or The Outsider. Instead, he had fabricated his own mythology about twenty million black outsiders—and she thought this typed him as a superficial outsider himself, at least as a commentator on the black scene.

But in addressing Bobby, he would have been an insider, one white college man and public figure to another; his chance to exert influence would surely have been irresistible. So he would have been more of a pragmatist than Baldwin, being sure to meet Bobby on his own ground. The Kennedys, Mailer said more than once, were magical because they promised to be better than they were; he might have seen himself helping them to develop, meeting Kennedy democratically on his level, rather than challenging him to ascend as Baldwin had. It represented the essential difference between them when it came to the game of politics.

For this reason, I saw the Baldwin-Kennedy meeting as a grotesque parody of what was happening between Mailer and Baldwin all the time. Bobby was Mailer without his genius; Mailer would have been incapable of playing high school principal with Jerome Smith. He might have challenged him as a fellow warrior, much as he tried to share the stage with Sonny Liston, but he wouldn't have demanded an experience solely on his terms. Challenging you was his way of paying his respects.

He challenged Baldwin yet again in a new collection of his recent pieces. Referring to Baldwin's old analysis of him, *The Black Boy Looks at the White Boy,* he said Baldwin "talked a great deal about himself and a little bit about me, a proportion I thought well-taken since he is on the best of terms with Baldwin and digs next to nothing about this white boy." That was a mean blow; he'd been hurt and he showed it. But it reflected his feeling about Baldwin; you can't be hurt in that way by someone you don't care about. He'd also pointed out a resemblance between them; that "proportion" could apply to both their works. They were both high on what Moravia had called subjective reality. They tended to see every subject through themselves; "I" was the chief character; if the proportion was balanced between "I" and subject, it was effective, but sometimes "I" took over and the subject, the point of it all, was pushed into a corner. In this, as in so much else, they were excellent reflectors of their times. Egocentricity ran as high as paranoia. But if you didn't deal with it, keep it under tight control, your work—your life—could capsize.

When Mailer assembled this new collection, John Kennedy was in the White House and several of the pieces in these "Presidential Papers" were addressed to him, but by the time the paperback edition was ready, JFK had been assassinated and Mailer wrote a new, very sentimental introduction. Kennedy, he decided, had been one of the few presidents who could have been an outlaw—a White Negro?—like Jefferson, Andrew Jackson, Lincoln, and Franklin Delano Roosevelt. "He was a good and serious man, one now suspects." Mailer said he wouldn't retract any of his criticisms—none of them had been devastating by Baldwin's standards—but he wished he'd given Kennedy's humor more credit. He told a girl at a party that Kennedy "was a man who could have become great or could have failed, and now we'll never know. That's what's so awful." In a time of great white guilt over the racial scene,

101

whites badly needed a contemporary hero: Kennedy was like a sacrifice to the gods. Now that a white leader, young and romantic, had been killed to lie alongside the dead black heroes, white guilt was a little easier to bear.

Mailer might feel this way; not Baldwin. His great shock came with the killing of Malcolm X. He was in London when the news came, and in an impassioned press conference, he blamed white supremacy for the murder, though most people at the time simply blamed the Muslims, with whom Malcolm had had a disagreement so fundamental and so violent that he was forced to leave and form his own group. His death certainly suited a lot of people. He had gone out to Africa and was seeking African and United Nations help in solving racial problems at home. He and Martin Luther King were seeking an understanding, groping toward not only an alliance between them but of all the poor and underprivileged, white as well as black. It was a prospect that scared a lot of people and put them in danger. Now Malcolm X was gone. It seemed to enrage Baldwin more than anything that had happened during the tragic last few years.

I took a visiting British publisher to meet Baldwin and we caught some of the backwash of his rage. Tony Godwin, then editor in chief of Penguin Books, was an enterprising little man with a sly sense of humor. He came from the working class and had a sharp sense of the ridiculous when it came to power circles in Britain. He was also keenly interested in the racial struggle in the U.S., seeing it through English eyes as essentially a class struggle. I assumed that Baldwin and he, having a lot in common, would get on well. The atmosphere was stormy from the moment we appeared. A black friend of Baldwin's recounted a humiliating experience he'd had in the Village; another detailed some of his bad times at the hands of prejudiced whites. They laid it on a bit thick for the visiting Englishman, but Baldwin merely sat nodding his head as if he were the amen corner. Godwin, misreading the intensity of the feelings behind the words, attempted to make a joke of it. He knew the Negroes had had a hard time in America, he said, but then so had the Chinese . . . He wasn't allowed to finish. The Chinese? Baldwin cried at him. The Chinese had come here voluntarily; we niggers had been forced here in slave ships. "I had to work in the galleys to get here . . ."

"You, Mr. Baldwin?" Tony Godwin said with keen English irony, not understanding Baldwin's strong sense of identification.

That did it. Baldwin swept into a long litany of oppression and ended the lesson by forcing Godwin to listen to a record of Nina Simone singing "Mississippi Goddam" from start to finish. It seemed an unbearably long record to me. I kept glancing from Baldwin's solemn, angry face to Godwin's red, bewildered one, and despairing of any communication across the lines. Was this the kind of put-down that haunted Mailer's dreams and explained why he was so careful not to leave himself open for it? At last, feeling responsible for Godwin and wishing to turn away Baldwin's wrath, I said, "Look, you're treating us both as just a couple of white men."

"Well," he said, "that's just what you are."

By that time some European film director had arrived to take Baldwin to dinner; we all went down in the elevator in gloomy silence and parted with hardly a word. Godwin made straight for the nearest bar and had a strong drink. "I don't understand why Baldwin was so *upset*," he said, as disappointed as a child. I tried to explain to him, but without success apparently, for years later, when I asked him for his version of the meeting for this book, he still claimed not to understand. "I made some idiotic remark comparing the Chinese to the blacks, though I can't remember what it was which upset James Baldwin and put me in the doghouse," Godwin told me. He could never accept that some subjects were not joking matters, at least in America; his sense of humor, finely attuned to England, often didn't work across the Atlantic. Nothing, in fact, separates the two countries even today more than the difference in their humor; the English love of irony and their own brand of straight-faced teasing are seldom appreciated in America, the land of the wisecrack. On that occasion Baldwin and Godwin had been talking in different languages, and they never met again before Godwin collapsed and died suddenly in his New York apartment. He had left Penguin and joined a New York publisher, and he had been astonished to find that some New York editors who had welcomed him as a visiting Englishman completely changed in their attitude when he appeared among them as a competitor. He would have had a sly chuckle at his memorial service in New York, for several of these former business friends, about whom he had felt very bitter, appeared as prominent mourners. Baldwin no doubt would have drawn a moral from it.

When I next met Baldwin, he didn't refer to the row with Godwin and was quite friendly. The incident might never have happened; this was another day, another mood. I met him at the home of Robert Lewis, a veteran theater director, and the other guest was Roddy McDowall, a movie actor. The conversation had mainly to do with show business and Baldwin showed great interest in all the gossip; this was another side of him. When I got up to leave, he did, too. He seemed to want to make a friendly gesture—perhaps the Godwin meeting was on his mind after all. Outside, he automatically looked for a cab, but I persuaded him, as it was such a pleasant late summer night, to walk part of the way back to his apartment. We strolled about thirty blocks down Third Avenue and then across town, for Lewis lived on the East side and Baldwin on the West. "This is the first time I've walked through the city for years," he said as if surprised at his own temerity, staring with wonderment at the passing people and stores and snack bars. He was so used to taking cabs, he said, that on foot in this violent city, he felt strangely defenseless before the onrush of experience in the streets. When I left him at the door of his apartment building, I had the impression he was surprised to have made it across the city without being mugged or at least accosted; he hadn't even been recognized.

I had received an invitation to a party given by a foreign correspondent at the United Nations and she had asked me to bring along Baldwin if I could. He was now the kind of famous catch New York society hostesses liked. I made a joke of it to Baldwin, expecting him not to be interested, but he said, "I'll try it. I haven't been to a party for some time." I also invited James Purdy, a novelist who had known Baldwin in his early Village days and hadn't met him since. Even if it was a dull party, they could enjoy a reunion.

When I arrived at the party, both Baldwin and Purdy were already there. Baldwin was the center of a group of white women who were accosting him with questions about race. His replies were accompanied by a good deal of finger wagging. I hoped he was enjoying it. Purdy, with the dignified, reticent looks of a world-weary bishop, was standing in a corner, surveying the other guests as if they were raw material for a novel. I tried to draw him and Baldwin together. I touched Baldwin's shoulder and he swung around and saw Purdy. "James!" he said, embracing Purdy rather flamboyantly. "How nice to see you!" And then, without even waiting for Purdy's reply, he turned again to face the audience of women and finish what he was saying. That was the end of communication between the two men. Whereas Mailer might have aggressively followed Baldwin and competed with him in front of his audience, Purdy, a much shyer, more private person, retired back to his corner and told me indignantly that Baldwin had insulted him by treating him in such a show business way. He soon left, courteously explaining that it wasn't my fault but he just had to get away. I tried to draw Baldwin aside again, but without success. He was in the middle of a passionate lecture and so I had to give up and let Purdy go. They had much in common as writers—Purdy's view of America was quite as unsparing as Baldwin's—but that night it was as if they had nothing in common as men. A difference in color didn't explain it; nor did their coming from parts of the country as different as Harlem and Ohio. As Purdy beat a hasty retreat to the elevator, I wondered if it was simply the price of fame and the role-playing it imprisoned you in; perhaps they were merely competitors to each other now.

The guest of honor at the party was Alastair Hetherington,

105

at that time editor of *The (Manchester) Guardian.* He had spent much of his time with white politicians in Washington, but he had little or no direct experience of the black scene. I hoped a talk with Baldwin might redress the balance. But it was Bobby Kennedy all over again. Hetherington eventually stood on one side of the room talking to a group, Baldwin on the other; Baldwin's group was much the bigger and the hostess sped from one to the other. Eventually Baldwin came to me—I had taken over Purdy's corner—and said in one of those stage whispers that was probably audible all round the room: "Bill, get me out of here." I accompanied him down in the elevator to get a cab. He sighed deeply and said, "They really don't understand, even now. What more do they want?" He asked me to meet him later in a theatrical bar on Eighth Avenue. I went back to the party; the remnants were now clustered around Hetherington, who was talking about Kennedy. One of the women who had been questioning Baldwin—didn't it occur to her that he might not want to be treated like a public speaker at a party?—remarked bitchily that Baldwin seemed very bitter.

That should have been a lesson to me, but it wasn't; I chanced another meeting. A woman I knew slightly at a publishing company invited me to meet some writers and I asked Baldwin if he wanted to go along. He said yes, since she was a friend of mine. Our group grew on the way, so we arrived at the woman's apartment building in the Village with James Parker, a young artist, and his two cousins, Marcella and Verbert, and Marcella's friend, Florence. In the elevator going up to her floor, an old white man demanded to know whom we were going to see. As we told him, it was none of his business, but he persisted rudely and aggressively, and Baldwin at last reacted angrily. We made it to our hostess's without a fight, but only just; the way we felt by then, it would have been a relief to fight and that's the way it might have been if the man hadn't been old and out of shape. Our hostess, knowing the old man and presumably his problems, was surprised to hear that we had taken him so seriously. But her tolerance seemed a luxury

106

to the blacks, to whom it was yet another occasion when they couldn't pay an ordinary social call on whites without going through some kind of inquisition.

The guests who had already arrived included some writers and teachers and an NBC journalist; they hailed "Jimmy" and immediately began to quiz him. I heard the NBC man, as if he was interviewing Baldwin on TV, ask pointedly if Baldwin didn't feel out of touch sometimes because in between his civil rights activities he lived abroad so much. Baldwin bristled and said angrily that he didn't need to be here all the time—he knew what was going on. It was obviously a sensitive point with him; his conscience probably told him he should be in the front line all the time, like the people down South, but he could survive as a writer only by getting away sometimes to do his writing. He sat, straight-backed and wide-eyed, as if he had the feeling that the NBC man was getting at him; coming so soon after the old man in the elevator, it was too much. After autographing a book for the hostess's son, Baldwin came over to me and used that stage whisper again, "Get me out of here."

So we were once more on our way, the five of us wending a slightly erratic course through the Village streets and across Washington Square Park, increasingly noisy and carefree like kids out of school, released from the earlier tension. Verbert, a large, cheerful girl, held hands and joked with Baldwin, making him seem by her side even smaller and slighter. We headed slowly for the Village Gate, where Baldwin had arranged to meet his mother and to hear Nina Simone sing.

I heard afterward that the NBC man's wife had remarked, "It just shows that no dialogue is possible between blacks and middle-class Jews." But that wasn't what it showed me; Jewish intellectuals were sometimes too self-conscious.

At the Village Gate, Nina Simone, accompanied by her husband like a bodyguard, came out to greet Baldwin and his mother, and he sent us all home in limousines. He was overgenerous, insisting on doing all the paying. It came out of all the years of poverty, of watching every cent; the meanest people I knew were rich, and they were always criticizing the extrava-

107

gance of their servants for buying a car or a color TV or going to Florida for a vacation . . . Baldwin's was this kind of "extravagance," and if he derived enjoyment from spending money on the people around him, it was one of the rewards for the hard years.

9

For all his apparent openness, his urge to tell all, Norman Mailer revealed little about his private self; his works were essentially "advertisements," not confessions, and as such, dealt mainly with the public role he had created—part aging rebel, part voyeur struggling for a piece of the action. If the Negro was an outsider trying to become an insider in American society, then Mailer was attempting to play a parallel role in the scenes he tried to take over. It was as though he was searching for some kind of comparable role to Baldwin's as an outsider—but in an arena of his own where he could start off with an equal chance.

In his Brooklyn Heights apartment, he showed me a model, seven feet high and built of twenty thousand pieces, that represented Mailer's idea of a city—a vertical city—of the future. If and when built, it would include 15,000 apartments for 50,000 people, would be more than half a mile high and nearly three-quarters of a mile in length.

Mailer pointed out these features with the smartness of a guide; he was obviously enjoying himself. He'd found a new role and also perhaps was rehearsing for his political future, for no politician could succeed in New York City without being an expert in city planning. If there was no nuclear war to put an end to us and the globe, Mailer told me, America would have to rebuild itself by the end of the century. Probably not one in a thousand of the buildings put up at the end of the nine-teenth century would still be standing by the end of the twentieth. But what would this new America look like?

Like most guides, he didn't expect an answer but was ready to give one. There was so much corruption and inflation in the building industry, real estate, and the unions, he said, that the result was not architecture to help us to live but graft, waste, public relations, and emptiness piled on emptiness. Our new buildings were as sterile, as flat, as operating tables. At the rate we were going, the whole country would look like Queens Boulevard, spreading a blank, faceless quality that seemed to have no character, no relation to any meaningful past, but merely represented our anxiety before the void.

The only possible solution, he said, to save some of the past and to avoid a megalopolis 5,000 miles long without shape or exit, was to build upwards. The city mustn't spread but instead must climb up to the heavens; he visualized cities with room for four hundred million people. He put his hand on the model. "And this is how it might look," he said proudly.

Mailer didn't leave it there; he had begun to have a master plan, a great general theme, into which all his ideas and activities could fit; his architectural dreaming was merely a part of his general view of the world that was Napoleonic—one of his favorite words about himself—in its ambition.

My diary noted: "Mailer went on to talk about his way of seeing the present as a time of plague; cancer was 'a metaphor' for his obsession. A disease even as major and mysterious as cancer was perhaps a last desperate attempt for the body to communicate that a function was seriously out of harmony. If our disease was averted by antibiotic or our pain was silenced by a sedative, Mailer said, then the attempted communication of the illness from one part of the body to the other had failed. The disease retreated into a bog of disharmony, and instead of one organ or two bearing the original stress, now ten organs shared a general tension, and we were close to the plague.

"We must resist the idea that disease is void of meaning," Mailer said, "for the next conclusion is that life is absurd." He told me—and this was the core of his argument—that it was the duty of each individual to free himself from that part of his life, his existence, which was born with the plague. Some of us succeeded completely in clearing our own plague and helping to clear the plague upon the world, and others only managed to clear their plague by visiting it upon other people, passing their disease into the flesh and minds of friends and other people nearby, and thus into the circuits of the world. This, for example, was how our huge, ugly, sick buildings came about— and he gave the model of his vertical city an approving pat. We had to get away from the present world of formlessness—it was as deadly as a whirlpool—back to a world of adventurers, entrepreneurs, settlers, and other egocentric types that helped to create a dynamic society.

Mailer stared through the large window of his apartment at downtown Manhattan across the water; it was as though he was watching the plague creeping toward him through the canyons between the skyscrapers. Could he roll it back, or was it as impossible as King Canute trying to roll back the waves? He seemed pleased, like an Einstein who had thought up the general theory of relativity and found that it explained many of our problems. . . .

I asked him if he didn't think the blacks in their present civil rights struggle had cleared their own plague and were helping to clear that of the world's.

He brooded over it, as if I was trying to test his theory. "Yes," he said. "In some cases. But not in all. Some blacks, like some whites, clear the plague from themselves by visiting it on other people. But," he added with a grin, as if he'd caught himself being too mean, too negative, too prone to the mood of the plague, "the blacks are doing more than the whites at present." It was obviously an admission that hurt him in some way; was it conceding too much to Jimmy Baldwin?

"That makes Baldwin a leading spiritual doctor against the plague—"

"A witch doctor," he said quickly. "Jimmy is able to contain such opposites in himself—that's his strength. He's certainly not a powerful man physically"—Mailer unconsciously flexed his shoulders—"but he has what amounts to a great power to survive. He has beaten the plague in himself and helped other people to deal with it. Like all good writers, he lives in a kind of dread; that's maybe why he travels so much. He's dealing with secrets of nature and it creates a special fear; you need a lot of nerve. Jimmy's work against the plague must inspire a very real fear, for he's not big or powerful. He must look easy to take if you don't know him, and he's saying very dangerous things that could bring a danger of retribution."

"From the plague?"

"From the plague carriers. But it's a risk we all run one way or another, to a greater or lesser extent." Mailer frowned with what Baldwin once described as his authoritarian look. "Jimmy's problem is that he misses the woods for the trees—that's always a frontline problem. You miss," he said like a general criticizing a sergeant, "the overall picture." He gave one of his sly Irish smiles. "Jimmy sometimes says ridiculous things—shows the pressure he's under. I don't think he believes there's one white man alive who has a genuine love for the Negro. He doesn't accept the fact that the Negro revolution has a profound meaning for whites, too. In one of our brotherly arguments, he said he'd rather spend his time with a white racist than a white liberal because he at least knew where he was with the racist. I told him he didn't seem to know the difference between a liberal and a radical—a liberal's someone who's not engaged, not serious. Sometimes I could slug Jimmy."

I imagined the contest—perhaps staged at Madison Square Garden. On my right, Norman Mailer, the Great White Hope; on my left, James Baldwin, the Black Champion—mentally if not physically heavyweight. By coincidence, not long afterward Baldwin was, if not in the same ring, at least under the same roof as Mailer. They were both at a meeting to question the Warren Commission's report on Kennedy's assassination. Mailer had already decided the Commission hadn't looked into everything and had distorted its hard findings. Baldwin, who had little faith in Establishment inquiries of any sort, would no doubt have agreed with him on this matter at least. So perhaps they were friendlier than they would have been otherwise. When Mailer came lumbering down the aisle, Baldwin slipped quickly out of his seat and met him head on. They exchanged a few words that seemed friendly, though also rather uneasy. Heads turned expectantly, waiting for their fight. They smiled confidently in one another's faces, measuring each other. Baldwin had long ago pointed out that they both tended to suspect others of putting them down, "and we strike before we're struck. Only, our styles are very different: I am a black boy from the Harlem streets, and Norman is a middle-class Jew." Harlem boy and middle-class Jew this time held their blows, perhaps for once trusting that the other wouldn't strike first. At least they parted peacefully, with amiable nods. Baldwin seemed curiously disappointed by the encounter. It was a no-contest, more like the weighing-in ceremony than an actual fight. They had sniffed around each other like two alley cats and then decided to leave it for another day. Great White Hope and Black Champion departed in opposite directions. But surely they would have to meet head on one day before they could be friends again.

Mailer, always a gambler with his talent, began to write a novel for *Esquire* magazine; it was fast serial writing in the great tradition of Dickens and Dumas. Astonishingly enough, the novel, *An American Dream,* dealt metaphorically with that great turning point in his life. For all his self-advertisements, he had never written of the stabbing before, except to hint that he had been a burnt-out case. *An American Dream* grew into a complex defense of a seemingly mad act—a decent man's murder of his wife. Madness becomes not abnormal, the reverse side of sane life, but integrated with sanity, as natural a result of certain experiences as an orgasm. And it should not be denied; it should be released. "Cancer is the growth of madness denied." Rojack, the chief character, resembles Mailer in several ways—a Mailer with some of his more far-out ambitions realized, a slightly idealized Mailer. Both went to Harvard, both met and made much of John Kennedy (Rojack once went out on a double date with JFK), both had political ambitions (Rojack was elected to Congress), both made violent attacks on their wives (Rojack killed his) and for a time both were held by the police, both were roughly the same age and were partly (Rojack) or wholly (Mailer) Jewish, both shared many of the same ideas and view of life (Rojack had earlier published a book entitled *The Psychology of the Hangman*).

Rojack tells himself, as Mailer might have done, "I've lain with madness long enough." Society might send you to Bellevue for a checkup, but in fact, since madness coexists with sanity, you just have to be careful to keep your balance. If you tilt too far through some extreme experience, then you must retreat and restore the balance; it is as though at such times, having gone too far, you must purge yourself of your madness and then become "something like sane again." If that doesn't happen, if the madness finds no outlet, it is "locked beneath. It goes into tissues, is swallowed by the cells. The cells go mad. Cancer is their flag . . ." And so we get back to the Mailer diagnosis of what's wrong with the world: it is the plague.

Mailer's hero gets away with murder; Rojack's madness finds an outlet, the cells stay sane and benign, untouched by plague, at the expense of his wife's life. And we are led to the conclusion, with all the author's authoritative style, that that is better than merely accepting the plague, lying down with it and passing it on. *An American Dream* seems to be a justification for Mailer's philosophy, if not for all his deeds, and it even includes a tribute to the Irish—they are said to be "the only men who know how to cry for the dirty polluted blood of all the world." Like many of the statements and insights of *An American Dream,* that's hard to justify on a realistic level, but as an allegory of Mailer's view of life, perhaps even as an explanation, however obscure, of his stabbing act of years ago, the whole novel is a fascinating apologia.

One of Mailer's ex-wives, not the woman who was stabbed, once claimed to see something of herself in the murdered wife, perhaps because the story was apparently brewing at the time she and Mailer were arguing their way toward a divorce. The wife's father in the novel, a millionaire figure of power (a plague-carrier), has been taken by some critics to be based on the Kennedy patriarch, but surely the character owes more to Mailer's grandfather-in-law, Lord Beaverbrook. Not in the superficial surface detail of his relationship to his daughter—whiffs of incest and all that, which make the hero's murder seem reasonably healthy and straightforward—but in his approach to power and its manipulation. Essentially the story is about the price of trying to break through all the power lines that tie down contemporary man; to escape, you may even have to commit murder; the alternative is to go mad, to succumb.

Sanity and madness—the self that survived was constantly fusing opposites. This was particularly true of a minority group in a society. A member of a minority group could be defined as one who "contains two opposed notions of himself at the same time." One's emotions were forever locked in the chains of ambivalence, Mailer said; the expression of an emotion forever releasing its opposite; the ego in perpetual transit from the tower to the dungeon and back again. By this definition, according to Mailer, nearly everyone in America was a member of a minority group, "alienated from the self by a double sense of identity and so at the mercy of a self which demands action and more action to define the most rudimentary borders of identity." But the leading minority group at present was the blacks (including Baldwin); was Mailer showing the way toward integration by recognizing that most of us belonged to minority groups (if so, it was close to Martin Luther King's attempt to unite all the poor, black and white), or was he in his own mind trying to cope with the blacks' superior position —Baldwin's advantage—by reducing its meaning to common alienation, suffered by others, too (including the Chinese of Tony Godwin)? Or, at the back of Mailer's mind, only half-expressed even to himself, was there the idea that blacks lived on the edge in white society and that to become free of the plague they might have to carry out an act of madness—a violent riot, for example, in their own ghetto? Was Baldwin therefore in Mailer's imagination now capable of an even more far-out act than his own?

One of the leading characters in *An American Dream* is black—Shago Martin—a singer, "an elegant Negro with a skin as dark as midnight." On his first appearance, he tells Rojack-Mailer, "Get your white ass out of here." The gauntlet was down: it could only end in a fight. And if everything was idealized in the novel, was this Mailer's dream of a confrontation between himself and Baldwin? Let's consider it that way, for in Mailer's work individuals carry the burden of representatives; Shago Martin couldn't only be himself; he was the black race and therefore he was Baldwin, too.

Shago-Baldwin swiftly draws a switchblade "like a snake's tongue." Rojack-Mailer refuses to be scared and Shago-Baldwin has to back down, blustering, "I'm too pretty to rumble," and "Haul ass, the black man is on the march and he won't stop until his elementary requirements are met." But no sooner does he turn his back than Rojack-Mailer, overcome by "a brain full of blood," suddenly attacks him from behind and stomps him down. He is tempted to let him go so that they can fight fairly, "but I had a fear of what I heard in his voice," and he goes on stomping him. "I was out of control, violence seemed to shake itself free from him each time I smashed him back to the floor and shake itself into me . . ." He throws him down the stairs: "Some hard-lodged boulder of fear I had always felt with Negroes was in the bumping, elbow-busting and crash of sound as he went barreling down, my terror going with him. . . ." But even then it isn't over; Shago-Baldwin crawls back to be beaten down again and again. Rojack-Mailer finally wins, but it isn't a satisfactory ending. He is too competitive—especially with Negroes as this was their time—not to feel pleasure in winning, even if he has taken unfair advantage of Shago (who cared in the jungle to be fair? To win was enough). Yet he has a hollow feeling, as if he had also lost something—is it a feeling he has really been doing the plague's work? Shago, crippled, struck in the back, has departed with a grace that makes Rojack seem as crude as the white racists down South, that seems to turn his victory into some subtle form of defeat.

His girl's attitude perhaps explains what was wrong. She—a white girl—has also been Shago's girl, and she has gone through all the pressures of being part of an interracial couple at that time. "You used to think the whole country depended on you and Shago," Rojack tells her jealously, and she agrees: "I used to think something would get better if Shago and I could make it." Rojack-Mailer might have vanquished his fear of the Negro, but there is some hidden ideal in integration he hasn't appreciated. The girl, brooding over her sense of failure, suggests that God is weaker for it and that the Devil—the plague—is that much stronger. And isn't Rojack-Mailer's winning dirty fight a victory not for him, not for an individual, but for segregation—the segregation of our separate selves as well as black and white? That way led to tilting the balance in favor of madness and the plague.

Although we are left with more questions and answers—and Shago's jive-talking Negro doesn't help in being almost like one of Mailer's White Negroes in black face—the final impression remains that the problem Shago raises is basically the same as the one Baldwin poses for Mailer; throwing Baldwin downstairs would certainly solve nothing between them. Just as a rationalization for Mailer's own far-out act has been dramatized and made as convincing as possible, so the antagonism, the rivalry, the hostility, the competition, and—dare I say it in the face of Shago?—the struggle for understanding between him and Baldwin has been idealized into a simple fight. Yet, in the end, it is not so simple or the victory wouldn't be so hollow. The loser seems in better shape than the winner. Is that a comment on the civil rights struggle? Or is Mailer, in spite of his own instincts, rejecting the old competition on which American society is founded, the very idea of winners and losers?

Even one's books were considered in terms of winners and losers. When *An American Dream* was published, the prestigious *Saturday Review* discussed Mailer's work in terms of success and failure: *The Naked and the Dead* was a success; *Barbary Shore* was an honorable failure; *The Deer Park* was "not

117

a success," and so on until *An American Dream,* which the reviewer, Granville Hicks, said he would like to believe was "a hoax," but concluded Mailer intended this story about "a projection of Norman Mailer's fantasies about himself" to be taken seriously. He quoted a fellow critic, Diana Trilling, as once writing that Mailer transcended the follies and excesses that attended hipsterism, and he wondered what she would make of this new novel, the strong implication being that Mailer hadn't transcended the follies and excesses this time. Writing in *The New York Review of Books,* Philip Rahv, another respected reviewer, found it "the most eccentric" of Mailer's novels; he thought the title was unjustified because it implied a generalization about the national life "palpably unsupported either by the weird and sometimes ludicrous details of the story or by the low-level private mysticism informing its imaginative scheme." It appeared from the novel that the way to "transcend" violence was to commit it, and he noted that Mailer nearly always identified with the perpetrators of violence, almost never with its victims. Rahv concluded—and it reminded me of Mailer writing about Baldwin—that if Mailer ever extricated himself from his entanglement with the hocus-pocus of power and the glamor dream of the romantic domination, both physical and psychic, of existence, "he might yet emerge as one of our greater talents." In other words, he would take Mailer more seriously if Mailer gave up the obsessions that made him Mailer. It seemed as though Mailer still had some way to go to re-establish himself in literary circles as well as in the public, political world.

He invited me to a party. I wasn't very keen on large parties, parties as events. I liked best the kind of party at which you could drift in and out, leaving when you got bored without offending anybody. That was why I didn't care for dinner parties; you couldn't leave until the end. But I couldn't ask what kind of party Mailer was giving. I knew him well enough, however, to suppose that guests would be performers in some Mailer drama. Instinct said to stay away; curiosity made me go.

By the time I arrived at the Brooklyn Heights brownstone, a crowd was already there, standing, sitting, lying on the floor. The big top-floor room overlooking the water and the panoramic view of downtown Manhattan was a fine place for a party, but some rope ladders hanging from a planked ceiling looked ominous to me. Mailer didn't mention them when he greeted me. He was beaming and benevolent, the perfect host. He introduced me to a few people and then I was on my own. Hemingway's widow, Mary, was there and Mailer beamed down at her on the floor; it obviously gave him pleasure, this Hemingway link—was she there to anoint him the successor? I remembered how Mailer had once sent "Father Ernest" an inscribed copy of *The Deer Park,* warning him "if you do not answer, or if you answer with the kind of crap you use to answer unprofessional writers, sycophants, brown-nosers, etc., then f—— you, and I will never attempt to communicate with you again . . ." And of course Hemingway never replied; the package came back from Cuba stamped with the Spanish equivalent of "Address Unknown—Return to Sender." At the same time he'd sent copies of the novel to other "established novelists and critics," such as Philip Rahv, Graham Greene, Cyril Connolly, and Alberto Moravia—and Moravia was the only one who answered. Mailer later described this literary politicking as "a silent shame" at a time when he was on the edge of many things "and I had more than a bit of violence in me." But at that party it was hard even to imagine the Mailer of those days; he and Mary Hemingway seemed on such good terms that surely "Father Ernest," if he had been alive, would have rushed to endorse *The Deer Park.*

Senator Javits and his wife, Marian, arrived. Mailer put his arm around the senator's shoulders, telling him some story that amused Mailer heartily—they might have been in the Senate cloakroom together. When he took Marian Javits to the window to survey the fine view, I tried to break the Mailer spell —to break out of a guest's sense of being in orbit around that powerful personality—by watching instead a well-known socialist writer sift through the other guests. He didn't seem to find anyone worth much of his time until he came to Senator Javits.

He spoke briefly to a small, poised man I had overheard talking in fluent French, and then he passed on. "Why did you drop Jean Malaquais so fast?" his wife asked him. "Malaquais?" he said, glancing back, concerned. "I'd have talked longer to him if I'd known who he was."

Mailer had once written that Malaquais was his mentor, that he had learned as much about writing from the Frenchman as from anyone alive, and that Malaquais had had more influence upon his mind than anyone he had ever known—from the time they had gotten well acquainted while Malaquais was translating *The Naked and the Dead* into French. For a mentor, he was staying very much in the background—I didn't blame the socialist writer for not recognizing him in looking for the celebrity guests. But then no doubt the relationship had changed since those days—Mailer was a mentor himself now to many people.

It had been at Malaquais' home in Paris that Mailer and Baldwin had first met, those "two lean cats, one white and one black," as Baldwin put it, circling around each other. Baldwin had noticed that between Mailer and Malaquais there was a good-natured but astringent running argument, with Mailer playing the role of the powerful but clumsy cub to Malaquais' old lion. Malaquais had taken Mailer to task for "The White Negro." Referring to "marijuana-soaked Hip," Malaquais said Mailer might be correct in stating that Hip and psychopathology followed two parallel paths, "but he has still to persuade this reader that the American Negro bohemian and his white imitator embody a special brand of the human species. Starting with the fact that the Negro's status within the American community is a marginal one, Mailer is not content to allow him his particular or characteristic psychological bent; he bestows upon him a Messianic mission . . ." In his reply, Mailer claimed Malaquais "would be hard put to find the taint of Hip without the blood of jazz." He added: "The Negro's experience appears to be the most universal communication of the West, and the authority of their tortured senses may indeed be passing by the musical states of their artistic expression, *without language, without conscious communication,* into the no doubt equally tortured senses of the wild sensitive spawn of two vast wars . . ."

Old lion and young cub: I watched for signs of this relationship, of their "running" argument running still, but Malaquais continued to remain discreetly in the background. When Mailer turned feisty and bade his assembled guests to take to the dangling ropes—I knew it!—I couldn't see Malaquais among the people who reluctantly began to obey orders. Had the old lion been excused or had he already clambered up out of sight? The well-known socialist writer was soon swinging halfheartedly on a rope, hardly moving, like someone in a summer hammock; he looked awkward and unhappy. Most of the other guests seemed to be responding obediently to the host's jovial orders.

Mailer's authoritative manner irritated me; summoned again to the ropes, I found myself remaining obstinately on the floor. The only other guest not airborne by then was a tall, grave man I had been told was a boxing manager. Mailer had Hemingway's respect for everybody related to boxing; perhaps that was why he left the tall, grave man alone and directed all his exasperated speeches at me. I remembered what Baldwin had said about "the belligerence of his stance, and the really rather pontifical tone of his voice." I knew at that moment exactly what Baldwin had meant, for here was the same Mailer standing before me, shorter but much heavier, more powerful. Baldwin had also been astonished that Mailer conceded so much to Jean Malaquais, that he thought so much of the French intellectual's opinion; Baldwin had remarked on how Malaquais had dominated his living room that time Mailer and he had first met. Well, in that, too, Mailer learned from Malaquais apparently, for he showed that he had every intention that night of dominating *his* living room.

He treated me as if I were a mutinous crew, hunching his shoulders as if he were about to bury his fist in my stomach,

121

although he was a heavyweight to my middleweight; addressing me in his imitation highfalutin English accent as if that was the way I talked . . . and then suddenly he grew tired of the contest and let me go—to hell?—rushing off to superintend the rope climbers. Some of the younger ones were as agile as monkeys, but on the whole the guests had no more athletic skill, gymnasium ease, than the average chair-bound city type. Mailer, however, walked beneath them, jovially encouraging them and giving fresh orders, every inch the skipper (of the *Jolly Roger?*).

It was impossible not to have a sneaking admiration for this wish to put his personal mark on a simple party, as if it were as much one of his creations as a book; he couldn't even do a routine act like lighting someone's cigarette without showing his own style. It was a Hemingway trait worthy of the heir apparent, for Papa Ernest had also tried to stage-manage reality. I was left with rather an unpleasant prissy feeling, as if I'd been a spoilsport; if Mailer had returned at that moment to press the attack, I'd probably have conceded defeat. But all he did was shoot a few evil glances at me from a distance, and that merely hardened my resistance.

I knew all about those glances of his from reading *An American Dream*. In the novel, he described how "my brain had developed into a small manufactory of psychic particles, pellets, rockets the length of a pin, planets the size of your eye's pupil when the iris closes down. I had even some artillery, a battery of bombs smaller than seeds of caviar but ready to be shot across the room." In *An American Dream*, Rojack-Mailer fired a battery of guns at a boxer who had made an insulting remark to his (and Shago-Baldwin's) girl; the boxer scowled as if "four very bad eggs had been crushed on his head." I felt as if Mailer had been firing some of those guns at *me,* so I scowled as if I'd been hit by his psychic power, too. And Mailer appeared to relax across the room, as pleased as if he were the winner in some obscure contest.

The next stage in the Mailer party game was to walk a narrow ledge high above the floor; resolutely I ignored the call to action and made small talk with the tall, grave boxing man about the view from the window; we both contemplated the beauty of Manhattan at night with the lights winking in some of the tall office buildings downtown—perhaps the cleaners were at work, we decided. All that time our host was rounding up people to walk the plank, for that was how it seemed, so narrow and high above the floor; one false drunken move and a person could fall far enough to get hurt.

Mailer was good-naturedly challenging his guests as if it were some ultimate test of courage; anyone who turned it down was chicken. When I saw him next, he was talking to Senator Javits and his wife, Marian. Surely Mailer wasn't challenging the senator in front of his much younger wife. It was a challenge many husbands would find impossible to turn down in their wives' presence, yet it was a risk that was not worth taking at the senator's age. With his political experience, the senator would surely be able to turn away any challenge, if that was what Mailer was talking to him about, without losing face.

Suddenly the senator stepped forward, watched by Mailer and Marian Javits. He wasn't a heavy drinker so there was no fear there, but his face looked nervous, uneasy, as if he was under great strain. Why the hell did he bother to do it if he felt that way? Mailer's watchful expression—surely there was a hint of a sly grin—irritated me and I fired one of his psychic guns back at him. I apparently scored a direct hit for his expression suddenly changed into a scowl—did he feel that bad eggs had been crushed on his head? The senator stepped forward with short, unsure steps, not looking down. Mailer urged him on. If I read the senator's face correctly, it seemed a long, long journey before he reached the end. Mailer clapped him on the back. Mailer's mind was capable of labyrinthine subtleties beyond my comprehension, and so I gave up trying to work out the meaning of the little drama I had just witnessed, but it left me feeling irritated with both Mailer and the senator, who at the very least had been encouraging our host in his game at our expense.

When I prepared to leave, Mailer rushed over, very upset. If I left then, he said, it meant his party had been a failure; it had *bored* me! He appealed to me to give it a little longer. "Be a good sport," he said in his awful English accent. He came on so strong I felt I had no choice but to stay. I couldn't understand why he was trying to keep me; I thought he would have been glad to see such an obstinate guest depart. I could only assume that he was such a competitive man that for his party to be a success all the guests had to be satisfied; *any* early departure was a judgment against him, a taste of defeat. His act with the ropes and the plank was perhaps only partly to satisfy his complex ego; it was also staged as an entertainment for his guests, to make them go away at last satisfied with an original evening, a good party at Norman's, a truly Mailerian occasion only he could bring to life.

I made conversation with some of the guests for another half hour. I remember one was a painter; I missed his name, but he talked as though he was famous. The host didn't stage any holding operation or even come over and talk, but he eyed me blankly a few times. I couldn't read his expression and was unsure whether he was shooting at me again or merely making sure I was staying. The spirit of the party slowly waned and at last I plucked up my courage enough to make another move to depart. Again Mailer rushed over, even more upset. But this time I was determined not to stay any longer, and when he saw that I wouldn't change my mind, he grew angry and acted as if I was insulting him. As I went down the stairs, he bellowed after me until I reached the street and disappeared, "I don't care if you didn't have a good time . . . I don't care . . ."

It was a damn lie of course; he plainly did care. I have never seen a host so worried about his guests' approval. As the night air cooled me down on the way to the subway, I began to feel that Mailer in fact had come out of the encounter much better than I had. He had really cared whether I found his party enjoyable, whereas I had been too sensitive, too critical—why couldn't I go along with him for an hour or two? Surely Mailer, even if he had been overly aggressive, had been more warmly human than I had. And then I caught myself; I was falling for that damned Mailer charm. Acting like an *enfant terrible,* he succeeded in making you feel guilty if you didn't go along with him. It was the same technique he used in his writing when he anticipated criticism by admitting to faults, mistakes, but in such a way—with such charm!—that he left you thinking not of the faults or mistakes but of how wonderful it was of him to be so honest.

I thought I'd never get another invitation to a Mailer party, but when his friend Jose Torres knocked out Willie Pastrano and became light-heavyweight champion of the world, I received an invitation to a celebration at Mailer's home. It was going to be a big affair, for Mailer had taken up boxing in a big way. He had even had a brush with Torres' opponent himself. Willie Pastrano told interviewer Peter Heller (quoted in Heller's book, *In This Corner*) that Torres himself was a very warmhearted guy, "but that guy he bums with, Norman Mailer, oh, man, he wanted to fight with me in the street. He wants to get beat all the time." No, getting beat wasn't Mailer's aim, he believed too much in winning for that. I remembered what Marilyn Monroe had said about him after I'd loaned her *The Deer Park*—he was too impressed by power; he'd obviously felt the way she had, she said: scared of being a loser. Mailer taking on champion Pastrano was the romantic tilting at windmills, the intellectual trying to show how tough he really was.

I could imagine what the Torres party might be like. I saw a boxing ring set up in Mailer's apartment for every guest to do time with Torres; I imagined Senator Javits putting on the gloves—and would I be able to avoid taking part this time? Again, instinct told me to stay away; curiosity urged me to attend. Trying to make up my mind, I drank with a friend in a bar, and finally had too many drinks to go anywhere. And what did it matter? Surely Mailer wouldn't miss me among so many other people. But I had forgotten his concern as a host at the last party; if he worried so much over your leaving after several hours, he certainly would notice that you hadn't shown up at all. I never received another invitation to a Mailer party.

10

Baldwin worried that his phone was tapped, that his apartment —seven rooms on West End Avenue and then part of a whole house on West 71st Street that he bought for his mother—was bugged, that casual callers were FBI informers. It was the price of fame in America, but especially of being involved in radical political activity—who of those in power could see the demonstrations and riots as merely a cry for simple justice?—and of wrangling with Bobby Kennedy.

I remember one evening calling in for a drink and finding ensconced in Baldwin's apartment an eccentric middle-aged white man who claimed to be a minister. After talking with him for a few minutes, I was convinced he was no more a minister than I was. Baldwin took me in his kitchen and whispered that he was sure the man was an FBI agent in disguise. I couldn't believe it, not fully appreciating the extent of Washington's paranoia about the black struggle (many white politicians were still trying to find Reds behind it all), and Baldwin got angry with me. I remember we had a pointless argument about Marilyn Monroe and Arthur Miller—Baldwin told me again how he had walked out of Miller's play, *After the Fall,* whose heroine resembled Miller's former wife, MM—and all the time we were watched by the "minister." I ended by becoming as suspicious or as paranoid as Baldwin. We couldn't wait until we'd got him out.

"Where did he come from?" I asked as soon as he went off into the night.

"God knows," Baldwin replied gloomily. "He just appeared."

Baldwin was always acquiring hangers-on in this way and then not knowing how to get rid of them; he was an easy mark for an FBI informer, if that's what the man was. Later it was established that Baldwin's phone *was* tapped, so perhaps we were right about the "minister," too.

It was at this time that an old friend of Baldwin's showed me a copy of his school magazine—the *Magpie* of DeWitt Clinton High School in the Bronx—of which Baldwin had been the editor. There were several choice Baldwin items: a short story, a few poems, and an interview with Countee Cullen, a leading black writer, who as a teacher had enthused about Paris and perhaps sown the seeds of Baldwin's later escape there. The innocence of the young interviewer back in 1942 provided a touching contrast to the fervent civil rights advocate of twenty years later . . . with his tapped phone.

Poetry, Countee Cullen explained to the young Baldwin, was "something which few people enjoy and which fewer people understand." A publisher published poetry only to give his company "tone." He never expected to make much money from it and seldom did.

"Yours truly," as the young interviewer called himself, "who had been under the impression that one simply published a book, and sat back and watched the shekels roll in, sat aghast. 'I never knew that,' I said. 'I guess a teaching job comes in pretty handy, then.' 'Yes,' he admitted. 'Also, I *like* to teach.' "

Countee Cullen suggested to the young Baldwin that in order for a writer to succeed, three things were necessary—read, write . . . and wait.

The young Baldwin asked him if he'd found much prejudice against the Negro in the literary world.

"Mr. Cullen shook his head."

I wondered what Baldwin himself would have replied to the question now. He frequently complained that for all his fame, he didn't get as big advances as some of the famous white writers, including, of course, Norman Mailer.

He also was no longer nearly as respectful toward his fellow black writers as he had been as a young interviewer. Lorraine Hansberry, when I met her, complained that Baldwin had treated the veteran black writer, Langston Hughes, very badly. Through talking with both of them, I was aware of some static between them. Langston Hughes had once described Baldwin as "the white-haired black boy of America." In a review of an early Baldwin book, *Notes of a Native Son,* in *The New York Times Book Review,* Langston Hughes said Baldwin's viewpoints were half-American, half-Afro-American, incompletely fused. Baldwin replied in a review in the same paper: "Every time I read Langston Hughes, I am amazed all over again by his genuine gifts—and depressed that he has done so little with them."

"Jimmy shows Langston no *respect,"* Lorraine Hansberry said. "He refers to Langston in public the way we niggers usually talk only in private to each other."

I met Langston Hughes at his home in Harlem—he'd lived there for twenty years, one of the few who'd remained in the ghetto after becoming famous. He said with a chuckle that when he received begging letters from people, he recommended that they address their requests to more famous writers like Baldwin. "People wanting to cause trouble between us repeat it to Jimmy and they say he's not amused. But I don't believe it. Jimmy has a good sense of humor, at least when he's not angry."

Langston Hughes, a round, brown, avuncular man with a jolly face, might not have become a Celebrity like Baldwin, but he was certainly famous. His baggage told the story. Back from Africa. Back from Europe. Back home on 127th Street, but not for long. Like the other established American Negro writers now in fashion, Langston Hughes was reaping the rewards of international invitations. But unlike most of the others, who belonged to the generation after his, he remembered when it all happened once before, and so he was enjoying this second experience of being fashionable without perhaps believing too much in it or gambling away his life on its remaining so.

"I've been twice lucky in enjoying a Negro renaissance," he recalled. "Negro literature was in vogue in the twenties when I was getting my start as a poet and now here it is again. But with this difference. The twenties were hung up on art. It was Negro art that people looked for. The present vogue is a by-product of the conflict over civil rights. The twenties' vogue grew out of the success of artists like Ethel Waters, Duke Ellington, and Louis Armstrong. The present one arises from the spirit of protest. James Baldwin and Leroi Jones, writers as protesters, have been in the center of it . . ."

Langston Hughes' weakness was that even when he was protesting, letting naked passion show, hardly anybody believed he was that serious. A joke or a flash of folk wisdom generally let us down lightly. Perhaps it was the effect of living through the First World War, the twenties ("There must have been two lynchings a week in the South"), the Depression, the Second World War, the Korean War, the Cold War, and the always-pressing racial conflict, and reaching his sixties and knowing that nothing anybody could do would work miracles and that a little acceptance was necessary unless you wanted to risk letting your anger consume you. Of course the danger of that attitude was that it was also the way of complacency and giving up. Sometimes Baldwin's anger seemed nothing more than his attempt to call himself to attention; maybe Langston Hughes tried to do the same thing with his humor— they had the styles of different generations.

I saw how wary Baldwin and Langston Hughes were of each other when they met unexpectedly in a West side restaurant that had been taken up by celebrities. Baldwin was accompanied by his brother, David, and a young white friend who had drunk too much and was noisy about it. David Baldwin took the friend outside to walk him around and try to sober him up. He returned just as drunk, staggering to the table, and it was obviously time he went home. Baldwin, who was usually relaxed and philosophical about such occasions, was strangely embarrassed, and when I asked what was troubling him, I was informed that Langston Hughes was sitting at a nearby table. It was as though his father had caught him in bad company; it at least reflected great respect. When we left, Baldwin went over to Langston Hughes and the two men, one black, one brown, one so slightly built, the other as round as an apple, shook hands and exchanged a few polite remarks. They both seemed extra courteous, in the way you are when you're uneasy with each other. Both extraordinary men, both eloquent spokesmen for the black experience in their totally different ways, they really had nothing to say to each other that night.

Was it because they were both writers, both famous, and felt some kind of rivalry that was even heightened by their both being black? Perhaps, but beyond that there was a personal side that had to be taken into account. The feeling of black for white, that underlying anger and bitterness that had to be overcome before any liking was possible, was simple compared with the feeling of black for black. That was as complicated as family feelings, as hard sometimes for outsiders—that is, whites —to understand as incestuous relationships.

The complexity of Baldwin's relations with fellow blacks was brought home to me by one particular experience. Until then, I hadn't realized how many enemies Baldwin had made in the Harlem ghetto by his early essays. When he was young and unknown, with absolutely nothing in sight to lose, he had written exactly what he thought in a way some middle-class blacks, particularly in politics and journalism and business, would never forgive, even years later. It's enough just to quote a few choice blasts from Baldwin's first collection, *Notes of a Native Son.* "One cannot help observing that some Negro leaders and politicians are far more concerned with their careers than with the welfare of Negroes, and their dramatic and publicized battles are battles with the wind . . ." Or: "The Negro press, which supports any man, provided he is sufficiently dark and well-known—with the exception of certain Negro novelists accused of drawing portraits unflattering to the race . . ." Or: "The best-selling Negro newspaper, I believe, is the *Amsterdam Star-*

News, which is also the worst, being gleefully devoted to murders, rapes, raids on love-nests, interracial wars, any item—however meaningless—concerning prominent Negroes, and whatever racial gains can be reported for the week—all in just about that order . . ."

Years later, when he wrote an introduction to *The Negro in New York,* a WPA history, old enemies were still lying in wait for him . . . as I found out to *my* cost. Several versions of the WPA history, written in the thirties by a group of black writers headed by the late Roi Otley, were lying in the Schomberg collection at the library on West 135th Street. None was complete; the last version, with pages missing, was not the final one, but had an editor's scribbled notes in the margin indicating revisions. It was a genuine Harlem document that had lain there for over twenty years and was important enough to be published even in its unfinished state; God knows Harlem didn't have that many historical documents of its own as most of its history had gone unrecorded.

The New York Public Library decided to publish it in collaboration with a commercial publisher, Oceana Publications. As I was working at the time for the Library's Director of Publications, Professor David V. Erdman, who was a student of radical politics as well as an authority on William Blake, I was given the job of getting the WPA history into print at long last. It wasn't going to make much money for anyone and so there was only a small budget. I approached some black writers and black academics in the hope that one of them would act as editor for a small sum within the budget. No one, however, seemed to see it as a labor of love; they all asked for fees I couldn't meet.

So in the end I had to put together a complete version myself. Mrs. Jean Blackwell Hutson, the head of the Schomberg Collection and a friend of Richard Wright's, agreed to write a preface, but when I asked for a temporary assistant to check some points, expecting some Harlem student might like the task—it could have brought some credit at college or in a job application; the history belonged to the ghetto so there was surely some pride in it—I was provided with a white woman who was certainly competent but who had no connection with Harlem. So that made two of us. I felt like saying, "This has lain around for twenty years, and when I asked some of you if you wanted to do it, all you could see in it was a fat fee. So I don't see that you've got any right to put me down if I try to get it done!" But that was too simple; the resentments went too deep. All a lot of people could see was another white man muscling in on something that belonged to them.

I hadn't approached Baldwin because I knew we couldn't afford his fee and I didn't want to seem to be asking for any personal favor. But he got to hear about it and wanted to know all about it—he, in fact, showed the kind of interest I'd expected in all the blacks I'd approached but hadn't found. He asked if he could help in any way; he would write something if I could use it. I told him he would be ideal to introduce it as it was basically a history of Harlem and he was a Harlem boy who had made good. He said he'd do it. I explained that a document of that kind could only have a small commercial sale and so our budget couldn't possibly meet his kind of fee. He shrugged. He understood that; he'd do it for nothing. And he did. In certain publishing circles Baldwin had a reputation for being erratic and not meeting deadlines. All I can say is that a long introduction arrived early, in perfect condition. He had found the history rather grim—grimmer than it intended to be; in the light of what had happened in the years since the book was written, it was a really appalling witness to cupidity and cowardice, he said. Some of it read almost exactly like Woodham-Smith's record of the Irish famine, *The Great Hunger.* But that story was over for the Irish, he said. How long was it going to be before you could say that for the blacks in America?

The only editorial change in what Baldwin had written involved a remark about Ronald Reagan, who was then governor of California. An editor at Oceana Publications worried that it might be libelous, though the redoubtable Professor Erdman wasn't bothered by it. Baldwin was asked about it and he immediately rephrased it, making it safe but no less stinging, and thus the book was ready for launching.

132

There was a publication day party at the Schomberg Collection to which countless black celebrities were invited, but to my knowledge, not even those who seemed to rush to every white premiere in midtown New York bothered to make it uptown to 135th Street. Baldwin was far away in Turkey (where he said he was lecturing on Henry James!) but he remembered to send greetings and regrets. He had shown himself to be very loyal to Harlem.

I was surprised, then, by what happened when the book was discussed on a Harlem radio show. Mrs. Hutson wasn't free to take part and she didn't come through with any black deputies, so that left me if we wanted to harvest some publicity for the book. The occasion was ironic from the beginning; I was involved in the reverse of the Harlem joke that downtown every black was mistaken for a messenger. When I went up to Harlem and presented myself at the reception desk and asked for the producer of the show, the black receptionist asked me if I had come to collect a package! I explained what I had come for and was then shown in to a back room where I was greeted by two men—a dapper little black man, who had the kind of smile it's impossible to read or to see past, a smile without humor—he was the host of the show. The other man was also black but bigger, plumper, older, and with a certain old-fashioned elegance.

Both men received me with surface friendliness but soon displayed an underlying hostility. The host allowed that he was puzzled by the choice of me—a white man—to complete the editing of a Harlem document. I explained why I had been stuck with it. "Oh," he said, and that humorless smile of his widened into a dazzling display of teeth, "you mean you did it simply because there was no one else who wanted to." The other man made a disparaging remark about Baldwin—what did he know about Harlem's history? I could imagine this was the kind of situation that Mailer had imagined himself in— alone among blacks and being put down as a white intruder. I wondered how he would have responded; even if I could imagine it, I wouldn't be able to do it. I hunched my shoulders like

133

Mailer and let my anger show. Look, I told the older man, who was going on sarcastically about Baldwin, I wasn't going to sit there and listen to Mr. Baldwin be insulted. He had written a fine introduction to this Harlem volume for nothing, which was a damn sight more than anyone else had done. If he—the older man—was so smart, why hadn't he got the history published before now? The host, seeing that he might be left with no show, made more of an effort to be courteous and eventually we got down to discussing the book. Their animosity showed a little but not enough to upset the show, and I got in a few sharp digs of my own, so at the end I felt the honors were even. The host asked me to stay for a drink, but that seemed to me beyond the call of duty.

When I next met Baldwin, I described my encounter. He asked who the older man had been.

"George S. Schuyler."

"Oh, my," Baldwin said, "I can see why it happened now. Schuyler doesn't like me and I don't like him. You got in the middle of it."

In *Notes of a Native Son,* Baldwin had referred to Schuyler's column in the *Courier* and had commented that Schuyler's "Olympian serenity infuriates me" but he reflected "with great accuracy the state of mind and the ambitions of the professional, well-to-do Negro who has managed to find a place to stand." Baldwin added: "Mr. Schuyler, who is remembered still for a satirical novel I have not read, called *Black No More,* is aided enormously in this position by a genteel white wife and a child-prodigy daughter—who is seriously regarded in some circles as proof of the incomprehensible contention that the mating of white and black is more likely to produce genius than any other combination."

In a later book, *No Name in the Street,* Baldwin described appearing on a television program with Malcolm X . . . and George S. Schuyler. Baldwin described the program as "pretty awful." Malcolm X and he "very quickly dismissed Mr. Schuyler and virtually everyone else, and, as the old street rats and heirs of Baptist ministers, played the program off each other."

Schuyler and Baldwin were not only of different generations but of different classes; they could never agree nor, it seemed, even afford to tolerate each other; sooner expect love between Cain and Abel than between conservative and militant blacks.

The Schomberg Collection was in financial difficulties and so Mrs. Hutson was keen to organize some help from prominent blacks. Baldwin and she had never met each other, and so I invited them out to lunch. Mrs. Hutson interested Baldwin, partly, I supposed, because she had been a friend of Richard Wright's and also because she knew some African leaders. Baldwin seemed to be edging toward Africa as if he had in mind a book *(No Name in Africa?)*. The *New Yorker* wanted him to write about some aspect of Africa (it had also offered him a television set so he could write some television criticism). Baldwin had been there on a visit with his sister, Gloria, and they had both been charmed because they had not always been spotted as Americans; they were even mistaken for Africans— from Dahomey.

Yet Baldwin was clearly in no rush to write about it. He had too subjective a view of reality to do a quick, easy journalistic job; he had to find a role to play himself—like Mailer—before he could describe any scene. He was obviously still trying to find his role that day he talked with Mrs. Hutson. They discussed Ghana and Nkrumah, whom she had known; they mentioned Richard Wright but quickly passed on; the Schomberg came up and both of them waited for the other: Mrs. Hutson seemed to have no proposal to make to Baldwin and he had no idea to put to her. I felt both were somehow disappointed in the other, not because they were hostile, far from it, but because they had given each other roles to play that they weren't playing. I remember over coffee they talked at last just about their families and then parted on the street, each to go a separate way. I walked down Seventh Avenue through the heart of Harlem with Baldwin. Several people recognized him; he might have been a movie star. What white writer would have been so easily recognized in his old neighborhood?

I had wanted Baldwin to meet an extraordinary woman on

132nd Street—Miss Gertie Wood from Guyana, where she had been awarded the Order of the British Empire for her work among children, and who now worked in New York as a cleaning woman for several white families. Her small room was crowded with books and Baldwin was her favorite writer; she had something of Albert Schweitzer's reverence for life and so she found it hard to kill cockroaches, and there were nearly as many in her room as there were books. Baldwin agreed to call on his devoted reader provided he could go by way of a barbershop and a bar. A Harlem barbershop is a social center as well as a place of business, and so cutting Baldwin's hair was a whole afternoon's work, ten minutes of haircutting and several hours of exchanging stories and ideas about the state of the world. Baldwin was clearly enjoying himself; he was back in the past not even as an unknown young writer but as a boy to whom these streets had been the whole world.

The next stop was Small's Paradise, a dim, agreeable bar where one of the other customers, a singer named Little Charles, sent Baldwin a drink to welcome him home. I kept phoning Gertie Wood that we were on our way, but by the time we made it, we were hours late and her dinner for us had been waiting a long time. It didn't matter, though. Baldwin settled easily among the books and the cockroaches and soon was learning from Miss Wood how to execute a perfect straight left, should he ever need it. Mailer, I felt, would have enjoyed that, too. Miss Wood explained to Baldwin why she had never become an American citizen. When she had arrived in Florida, she had run into heavy racial prejudice, and she felt she could not become an American if that meant she would then be treated officially as "a nigger." She had left Guyana because her parents and her sister had died and she could not bear to go on living there, reminded of them wherever she moved. She obviously found it easy to talk to Baldwin and he responded with great warmth. I wished Mailer could have been there—for other reasons as well as receiving a boxing lesson from Miss Wood. His concept of The Negro, of the black experience, of black life, could do with more Miss Woods and fewer Shago

Martins. (Speaking at a meeting downtown, Baldwin had been asked what he thought of Mailer's idea that blacks had better sex lives than whites. Baldwin had said carefully that Norman must have been joking. No, the questioner obviously felt that Mr. Mailer was serious; well, Baldwin refused to take it seriously.)

I remember when we left Miss Wood's we went back to Small's for a last drink and Baldwin began to talk gloomily about Lorraine Hansberry. She had just died, at thirty-four, of cancer. It was impossible to think of that articulate, impulsive, so-alive young woman as dead. Baldwin had visited her for a last time in the hospital shortly before she died. She couldn't speak, so she smiled and waved. He remembered how he had learned she was seriously ill. He had met her and complimented her on how beautiful she looked. He remembered saying, "Lorraine, baby, how in the world do you do it?" And she smiled and said, "It helps to develop a serious illness, Jimmy!" and then she'd waved and walked off.

"We had such arguments," Baldwin recalled. "Knockdown drag-out fights about history. 'Really, Jimmy,' she'd cry. 'You ain't right, child,' and then she'd try to put me right, straighten me out. Sweet Lorraine." When he wrote about her, he said they had the kind of respect for each other "which perhaps is only felt by people on the same side of the barricades, listening to the accumulating thunder of the hooves of horses and the treads of tanks." Baldwin told me that the only person he knew of that Lorraine Hansberry couldn't get through to was Bobby Kennedy. "She was trying to tell him that the hooves of the horses and the treads of tanks were no respectors of persons, and he didn't understand. He wanted it nice and tidy and politically advantageous. And Lorraine wouldn't let him get away with it—any more than she would let me get away with things if she thought I was wrong."

Baldwin tended to see the "barricades" everywhere and he was probably right. He had a play on Broadway, *Blues for Mr. Charlie,* which was dramatic enough, God knows, as it dealt harrowingly with the return of a young black man to his home

137

in the South and his betrayal by a white liberal, but to Baldwin the struggle around the play's presentation and to keep it running was a much greater drama; he treated it as if he were personally in a wrestle with the white world, like Jacob's wrestling with the angel. First of all, long before the play ever reached rehearsals, one famous director after another was supposed to be going to direct it. Elia Kazan was said to want it for the new Lincoln Center theater. Then Kazan was out of the plans and someone else was in. Shouldn't the director be black, since the play dealt with the subtleties of black experience? Who was money-in-the-bank to the backers? Come to think of that, who were the backers?

When I saw Baldwin then, he had nothing but the play on his mind; he could talk about nothing else. He was completely self-centered for a few hours. His clothes also seemed to have changed, to have become more theatrical in color and style. He would tell me about something to do with the play—often trivial—and then would solemnly add, "Don't tell any of your reporter friends." Burgess Meredith, a lively little man and a clever character actor, was often in the group sitting around Baldwin's living room. I gathered that Meredith was the latest candidate for director, though some were against him because he was white. He and I discovered a common enthusiasm for the late Alexander Woollcott, the gifted journalist and formidable literary personality. The young blacks in the room, who were of a generation after Woollcott died, seemed to think we were having a white conversation they couldn't share, and it didn't enhance Burgess Meredith's qualifications for directing the play in their eyes. But Baldwin himself obviously approved of Meredith and I wondered whether it might be because Baldwin thought he could manage Meredith, that he could pull rank over him in matters of black experience, and might even get to direct the director. Most authors are merely tolerated at the rehearsals of their plays, but Baldwin could no more take a back seat than Mailer could; I knew he had an urge to make movies and I was sure it now extended to directing plays.

The Actors Studio, center of The Method, was presenting

138

the play, and soon Baldwin's wrestle with the white world localized itself into a struggle with the heads of the studio, Lee Strasberg and Cheryl Crawford. Strasberg—short, didactic, with the aura of a Freudian prophet—and Crawford—smart, laconic, with an air of having no illusions—provided a perfect contrast to the slight, intense, finger-wagging Baldwin. His sense of mission clashed with their sense of theater; Burgess Meredith as director would be in the middle.

One problem was that the play, a long one, had to be cut; another was that Baldwin wanted his brother, David, in a major role. David Baldwin, taller and heavier than his older brother, was a talented, realistic man who had had little acting experience and admitted it. He didn't want to be the cause of any arguments and offered to quit. Baldwin wouldn't hear of it, and eventually David stayed, did well, and the argument found other grounds. Baldwin occupied Junior's Bar, near the theater, during rehearsals and he and Strasberg sparred at long distance. Baldwin thought The Method an appalling way of working that "has nothing to do with acting." Such remarks trickling back from Junior's obviously won him no love at the studio. It was as though Baldwin couldn't function at that time as a writer without seeing his work as part of the general struggle; otherwise he was merely playing, taking time off while others were beaten up and jailed. Strasberg became a kind of mythological white Southern sheriff who was getting in the way of his telling the truth, and The Method was comparable to some tight-assed WASP religion.

The clash didn't end with opening night. The play received mixed notices and then it was a struggle to keep it open. A one-week closing notice went up and then was taken down. Baldwin's apartment became a factory for leaflets, posters, signs, all kinds of advertisements and publicity messages; donations rolled in from white liberals and blacks happy to see a black play on Broadway for once. Lucien Happersberger, who had known Baldwin in his Paris years—"We used to meet once a day and pool what we'd got," Baldwin told me—and had later been his business manager, became friendly with one of the stars of the play, Diana Sands, and married her. Baldwin, in his worked-up state, obviously felt he was losing a friend at a bad time; he needed all the friends he could get against the enemy.

"I remember Lucien when he first came to New York; we arranged to meet in a Harlem bar, and when I got there, Lucien had already made himself at home, chatting to the barman and the customers." Baldwin told that story with wonderment; Lucien had broken the racial barrier; and now here he was marrying a black girl.

I watched Baldwin clambering up a tall ladder to make some point about black experience to Burgess Meredith. At times the director looked as though he felt like a white liberal being conned by streetwise blacks, an experience I was sure that still haunted Mailer's dreams and explained why he was careful not to get so involved. But Meredith, a canny man of the theater whose floppy hair and big eyes were like a disguise, probably took what he needed from all the black advisers around Baldwin and left the rest; at least the production had a coherent style. But its days were clearly numbered, in spite of all the rescue attempts.

Baldwin talked as if its closure would be a triumph for white racism. "I wanted to upset people with this play and I did, and that's why they're trying to close it. It's based loosely on the case of Emmett Till—the Negro youth who was murdered in Mississippi in 1955, a case that has haunted me, bugged me, ever since. What is almost hopeless about such racial crimes is that the people who commit them dare not see how terrible they are, for it would drive them mad, and so they blind themselves to it and go on repeating it. But we have a duty to understand such murderers—I still hold on to the idea that we're all brothers in spite of everything that's happened!—and we must stamp out this plague that drives people to murder before we are murdered ourselves. When I was writing *Blues,* I also had in mind Medgar Evers; I knew him and visited with him before he was murdered in Mississippi. With such memories, it would be easy to suppose we're sentenced to remain in such darkness forever, but I refuse to believe it, and so I wrote this play to try to understand, to testify to the power of light . . ."

Baldwin didn't wait to see the play close, but left the country; it was as though he couldn't bear to witness the end of it after such a long, hard struggle, for that meant the enemy had won and he was the loser. That hurt his competitive spirit as much as it would have hurt Mailer. He chewed over the whole experience in his next novel, *Tell Me How Long the Train's Been Gone,* much as Norman Mailer had brooded and fantasized in *An American Dream.* Baldwin's novel was written in the first person by a famous black actor, Leo Proudhammer; it was as much Baldwin's idealization of himself as Rojack had been Mailer's. The boy preacher carried to an extreme, the poor Harlem boy behind the mask of fame; the novelist's magic wand had transformed him into a handsome theatrical star, Baldwin as Sidney Poitier.

Yet Leo Proudhammer in his essentials was still very much Baldwin. He was fighting again the battle of *Blues for Mr. Charlie;* this time, however, the stage was not in a narrow theater but in the never-ending streets. Baldwin, who had nearly driven himself into a nervous breakdown over the play, began his novel by imagining that the great strain had been too much; Leo Proudhammer had had a massive heart attack. The battleground was complete even to an actors' studio dominated by a didactic character named Saul who analyzed the students' performances much as Lee Strasberg did. There was a confrontation between Saul and Leo in which Saul doubted Leo's talent and described his performance as "bombastic, hysterical, and self-pitying." So defenders of the Actors Studio had described Baldwin in the heat of battle. But Leo emerged the more sympathetic character in the end; Saul was made to seem cold and even rather smug and destructive. Baldwin had his revenge for the closing of *Blues.*

Another aspect of the novel was the closeness of its ideas to Mailer's. What separated the two men now had never seemed so slight and unimportant compared with all that they had in common. Leo Proudhammer's heart attack was comparable to

141

Rojack's release into madness; both were the means of a return to health, to sanity, to a natural balance. Baldwin even saw the same "plague" threatening us that Mailer did. He had set *Blues for Mr. Charlie* in Plaguetown, USA: "The plague is race, the plague is our concept of Christianity: and this raging plague has the power to destroy every human relationship." Now, in *Tell Me How Long the Train's Been Gone,* Baldwin wrote: "I had conquered the city: but the city was stricken with the plague. Not in my lifetime would this plague end . . ."

Both Baldwin and Mailer now saw the same symptoms, only their diagnoses were different. Baldwin saw racial prejudice where Mailer saw cancer; was it merely semantics—or was it a difference in experience?

11

Norman Mailer, too, had a play produced and waged his own battle of survival. It probably irked him that Baldwin had his play produced prominently on Broadway, whereas his own adaptation of *The Deer Park* failed to find Broadway backing after years of trying. He had to settle for an out-of-the-way off-Broadway home at the Theatre DeLys.

It was an old play that had originally run for four hours; Mailer had had grandiose dreams for years of the Greatest Broadway First Night of the Decade, had declaimed to himself in a rage of rejection that his play was as good as those Broadway classics, Arthur Miller's *Death of a Salesman* and Tennessee Williams' *A Streetcar Named Desire,* and finally had had to accept the fact that if he wanted to see it performed and done right, he would have to settle for comparative obscurity off-Broadway. It was a hard decision to have to accept—a half-defeat from which he had to wrest a victory to be content.

Being Mailer, he didn't wait for reviewers or audiences to decide for him. He went on the offensive, challenging every aspect of the theater—the Broadway theater that had rejected him—and thus played a new role: the playwright as critic. Like Baldwin, he related his struggle to have the play produced, and kept running, to his larger themes and the way he saw the world. The forces against his play were not the racial ones Baldwin had seen, but symptoms of that same general plague he found appearing everywhere. The theater, cohabiting with dehumanizing TV, was "close to an excruciating death by long wallowing, for the smelting operations will enlarge, and the big houses will continue to be filled with armies of pill-fed human-oids in for the night from television. The Theatre of Manipula-tion will swell in every joint. It will thrive like edema. And the critics will be the doctors who call this swelling, health. For it is true. To talk of Broadway is to talk not of amusement but disease . . ."

Oh, Broadway, reject Norman Mailer at your peril! How monumentally impossible for any drama reviewer to review Mailer's play to his own satisfaction (or Mailer's!) an hour after he'd seen it—which was the task of the morning paper drama reviewers—when Mailer had lived with the events and themes for close to eighteen years, had worked on the play for ten years, had rewritten it four times!

Having anticipated and answered any bad reviews, Mailer proceeded to explain what reviewers should see. His play was an existential work about sex and love, and the no-man's-land between them that alters in the night. It lay between the explorations of the realistic play and that electric sense of transition which lived in the interruptions and symbols of the Theatre of the Absurd.

Mailer might have saved his effort. "My old friend" *Time* magazine referred to "unearthly depravity," whereas the *Wall Street Journal* found the play "a blast of fresh air." Mailer found the reviews generally condescending, treating "a flam-boyant and somewhat over-rated novelist" as an apprentice playwright. Yet, even if the reviews missed his point in their rush to print, the play, Mailer said, was a hit—not a smash hit, but nevertheless a hit. He was a winner; the play ran for four months. From the security of success, he looked at Broadway audiences and the plays that had made it on Broadway and found symptoms of the plague behind every box office, on every stage, in every auditorium. The conclusion seemed to be that not only was *The Deer Park* a unique work of a complexity rare in the New York theater but that it had been lucky not to make

144

the deadening atmosphere of Broadway; it had grown instead in the fresher, more creative air of the Village.

I went to see Mailer's play soon after it opened with two friends, James Parker and Baldwin's youngest sister, Paula. When we came out at the end, Mailer was in the lobby surrounded by young Village intellectuals and he was obviously enjoying answering their intense questions about the state of the theater today. He had put on some weight since I'd last seen him and had acquired an avuncular smile. I asked Paula if she wanted to go over to talk to him, but she shook her head; I sensed that she didn't see him as a friend of her brother's, and the Baldwin family was intensely loyal to their famous member (though when people gave her eldest son special attention, Mrs. Baldwin insisted that all her children were equally important; she had no favorites, even if the world had).

While he was enjoying this heady aftermath of *The Deer Park*'s production, Mailer also made a full-length underground film. It was inspired by after-performance gatherings at a Village restaurant named Charles IV, at which Mailer and a few others played a game of imitating members of the Mafia, talking like dons. They became so clever at it that Mailer decided it would be a good idea to bring in a cameraman to record half an hour of their exchanges. From this modest suggestion grew a movie entitled *Wild 90*, filmed on four consecutive nights with $1,500 worth of film. There were no retakes, no script. Mailer claimed that it had more obscene language than any film ever made ("Obscenity is where God and Devil meet . . ."); he also said it was one of the first existential movies, making it a near-relation to his existential play. He saw its realism, well revealed in its use of earthy, obscene language, as helping to bring together the two separate parts of American society, as separate as the lobes of a brain. The Establishment would never narrow the gap between itself and the so-called "deprived" until its knowledge of the other was accurate rather than liberal, condescending, over-programmatic. Eye-opening works like *Wild 90* had this kind of accuracy, according to its maker.

If Baldwin had made *Time*'s cover and Broadway, Mailer

was ahead in the film world. There had been many flirtations between Baldwin and Hollywood, but none yet had led to an actual movie. Baldwin had adapted *Giovanni's Room,* hoping for both a Broadway and a Hollywood production. Elia Kazan had been interested in *Another Country,* but Baldwin told me Kazan had wanted to concentrate on the last part of the novel, the affair between the dead hero's sister and the young Italian-American, a love story about white innocence/ignorance and the black struggle for survival. Baldwin thought this too restricted a view of *Another Country;* it left too much out of what had led him to write the novel in the first place, and he said it was all or nothing. I attended a presentation intended to raise backing for a movie of Baldwin's short story, "This Morning, This Evening, So Soon," but nothing came of it. David Baldwin tried to create some interest in another Baldwin short story, "Sonny's Blues," about two black brothers who take different routes out of the ghetto; there was a perfect role for David in it, but nothing came of that, either.

Hollywood lived on half-promises and proposals that in the end seldom led to anything concrete. Until you had a written contract and some money, you could count on nothing. Baldwin's movie experience so far had been full of disappointments. Now that he was such a well-known militant spokesman for a cause considered radical, it was even more unlikely that the conservative, fearful film world would touch his work. This was the real cost of his civil rights activities—the loss of what might have been if he had kept his mouth shut and maintained a low profile. It was a price he was apparently quite willing to pay.

No one could accuse Mailer of having maintained a low profile or of keeping out of trouble, but he had not committed himself in anything but principle to the civil rights movement. His radical activity was strictly personal; if he had acquired an oddball reputation—this side of acceptability in recent years—it was not the kind that scared off many Hollywood backers. It fitted, in fact, a businessman's romantic idea of the writer as an Eccentric, an *enfant terrible. The Naked and the Dead* had been filmed, so had *An American Dream,* but the novels had been de-gutted and the results had been rather feeble, run-of-the-mill commercial movies that didn't represent Mailer in any true way. They must have been great disappointments to him; it was like making it to Broadway and then getting the off-Broadway treatment, a winner treated like a loser. No wonder he had wanted to have a try at movies himself; in his own eyes, he could hardly do worse and, given his aggressive self-confidence, his willingness to take a risk, to try new approaches, surely he could do a lot better.

Wild 90 had a very mixed reception and failed to achieve any wide commercial distribution. Most of its critics found it as incoherent as life itself, like trying to turn a tape recording of a barroom conversation into a novel. With some reviewers, this was cause for praise; others saw it as proof that Mailer was a mere apprentice at making movies.

But at least he had done it; Baldwin must have been envious of that. Baldwin's early "morbid desire" to own a sixteen-millimeter camera—that was what Mailer had used for *Wild 90*—and to make experimental movies was still with him in some ways. I spent a couple of hours with him at the Cedar Tavern, an old artists' hangout in the Village, and then we walked by a friend's house on 16th Street. Along the way, Baldwin suddenly stopped and studied a row of old brownstones and then put his hands to his face as if he was looking through a camera at them. "I'd forgotten," he said, "how photogenic certain corners of New York are—just as much as parts of Paris." He had recently seen the French movie, *La Guerre est Finie,* about a revolutionary twenty years later. I imagined a similar movie about American black militants. "Not now," he said. "In the seventies." I quoted Robert Frost's lines about not daring to be radical when young for fear of being conservative when old. Baldwin didn't laugh; he looked suddenly grim. "I wonder if we'll be like that," he said and then shrugged and changed the subject—back to the photogenic houses, I think, though there's no note about it in my diary.

It wasn't only Hollywood that flirted with Baldwin's movie ambitions; individual film people with white liberal sentiments,

147

eager to do something for the cause, often discussed possible movies with civil rights leaders, and sometimes Baldwin was drawn in as a potential scriptwriter, though I'm sure he also imagined himself as the director, if not one of the leading actors. A strong urge to perform, and some show business ham, (which helped the boy preacher and the man public speaker) was strong in him and sometimes distracted and fought with the other side of him—the writer. A film made independently offered the possibility of a collaboration between the two sides of him, performer and writer, much as Mailer had managed in *Wild 90.* So he was always willing to discuss such movie proposals, though as more and more of them never got past the first intense, ambitious exchanges, his hopes could never have been high.

Marlon Brando was an old friend of his from the early days in New York: Brando the fledgling actor and Baldwin the fledgling writer (and actor, too?). Later, when Baldwin took his desperate trip to Paris and was down and almost out in the streets, he sent an SOS to Brando, who by then had begun to have some early success. "Marlon sent a magical five hundred bucks," Baldwin told me. After nearly twenty years he still remembered his vast relief on receiving the money, for it had made life possible again. Brando as a young man had been a rebel without a cause except himself; now a rich man, he was nagged into liberal causes by the old rebel inside him. He wanted to do something big and effective for the civil rights movement; he suggested a movie with himself playing a violent and prejudiced Southern sheriff.

By chance I went by Baldwin's apartment when Brando was there to discuss his idea with some civil rights leaders, with Baldwin as host and middleman. Those taking part included Stokeley Carmichael and James Forman, two of the youngest and most militant leaders, who were closer to Baldwin's beliefs than some of the older black representatives. I had seen both of them in action in the South; they had come out of the Freedom Riders and the Student Non-Violent Coordinating Committee, the racy cavalier group known as "Snick." I had once followed Forman's attempt to open up the segregated lunch counters of Nashville, Tennessee. He had been a rude and irascible leader with the few white liberals who had joined the march from a black Baptist church to the lunch counters, all of which closed as soon as the chant of "We Shall Overcome" was heard. He was under great strain, since he was responsible for the strategy and the way it was carried out (inevitably it would lead to beatings and rough times in jail), but he also seemed to show a genuine dislike, bordering on contempt, for the few whites taking part. Like many black leaders, perhaps he suspected they were on an ego trip.

Now, in Baldwin's apartment, I saw both him and Stokeley Carmichael eyeing Brando skeptically. Brando's international reputation as a movie actor—for some, a great actor—obviously didn't impress them; nor did Baldwin's high opinion of him. They were clearly making up their own minds, these two veterans from the front line, and they threw some hard questions at Brando as he sat impassively on Baldwin's couch, beneath a painting of a black kid snowballing, a fine work by one of Baldwin's friends from the Paris days, the American artist Beauford Delaney.

Yet they were much more relaxed than when I had seen them in the South; there was a feeling of being on leave from the war. Forman could even joke about that time in Nashville and he asked me if I had the address of a mutual friend from Georgia who was teaching in Africa; the strain was obviously off for a few hours and he could think about other more personal business. It suggested he didn't take the proposed movie too seriously.

Stokeley Carmichael was younger and more dramatic; he had something of Baldwin's and Mailer's flair for getting publicity. It was he and his generation who had rejected the word "Negro," insisting on being called a black instead. And "Black Power" and "Black Is Beautiful" suddenly became their slogan. Under any other circumstances, it would have seemed ridiculous, like chanting that "Grass is Green," but the years of brainwashing under segregation had had their effect—an obvious example being the straightening of black curly hair into a white style. The aim of the civil rights movement was not only to break through the barrier of segregation but to undo the years of brainwashing. Young blacks suddenly began to grow immense Afros, to cultivate everything about themselves that was different. It was a time when African states were winning their independence from white colonial countries; many young blacks began to imitate not white styles but African, and to call themselves not Negroes or blacks even but Afro-Americans. Some of the older civil rights leaders seemed to be surprised by the changes; it was the younger ones, like Stokeley Carmichael, who pushed this particular breakthrough for black pride, for black power, against the years of brainwashing.

But that day in Baldwin's apartment, Stokeley Carmichael made no attempt to use his talent for taking the center of the stage; he didn't try to compete with Baldwin and Brando. He sat quietly listening, nodding, his long legs stretched out, chuckling when Brando did his Southern sheriff act. His presence was felt all the time, however, and when he rose casually to get a glass of water, all eyes followed him across the room. Brando, recognizing his power, suggested Stokeley might play himself in the movie. Stokeley thought about it, but didn't commit himself; at least he didn't laugh at the prospect of being a movie star as he might have done down South among the Snick people to whom nothing and nobody were sacred. He showed Brando the respect of taking him seriously. Brando did seem deadly serious—talking about schedules, when he would be free to make the film, that sort of humdrum, convincing detail, though with actors I was never sure when they were performing and when they were not. Baldwin watched Brando with an encouraging smile, raising no questions, no doubts. I had seen show business stars, white and black, spend a night down South raising funds for those in jail and then go back up North and talk as if they had been through hell and were lucky to have returned alive; they were dramatizing themselves as heroes and they should have heard what some Snick members said about them. I wondered if Brando was involved in the same kind of ego act; only time would tell whether the movie was ever made. Maybe I looked skeptical, because I heard Brando ask Baldwin who I was. Baldwin said something friendly so Brando gave up regarding me with his Southern sheriff expression.

He was trying to play a much more active role in the black struggle than most white celebrities; Mailer, by comparison, remained much more detached, even aloof. Brando surely had as big an ego as Mailer and wouldn't relish playing second fiddle in an essentially black scene any more than Mailer would. Was it that he was less realistic and believed that he could still play a major role even though he was white? Or was there something in his background, his experience, that led him to identify more closely than someone like Mailer? I mentioned it to Baldwin, but he was completely approving of Brando and beyond looking at his motives objectively; he was far less demanding of him and far less critical than he was of Mailer. Yet in this question of why Brando identified with the black struggle more than most white celebrities lay some key to the Baldwin-Mailer relationship through the years. Why Brando and not Mailer? I didn't know the answer. Not yet.

We all attended a Snick reunion outside New York at the home of Gordon Parks, the black photographer, writer, and movie director. He had written an autobiographical novel, *The Learning Tree,* and then made a movie of it—a movie that proved both a critical and commercial success. He must have awakened envy in Baldwin's heart. Stokeley Carmichael and Marlon Brando, free of the restraints of their more formal business meeting about the movie, showed themselves to be carefree dancers. Baldwin was also in a festive mood, making up in enthusiasm what he lacked in ballroom skill; everybody told his or her favorite story about Southern cops.

Not being much of a dancer and beginning to feel the strain of trying to keep up with Baldwin and his entourage, I wandered around Gordon Parks' pleasantly sprawling home and found our host, with his graying hair and melancholy eyes, contemplating the moon, all alone.

"A good party," I said.

"They deserve it," he replied; he knew what the Snick people had been through down South.

He was a short man—why did well-known people always seem bigger than they were? Brando, who seemed towering on the screen, was short. Baldwin was, too—and Mailer. Sometimes, however, the magic didn't work. I met Warren Beatty, fresh from his success in the popular movie, *Bonnie and Clyde,* and although physically taller than Baldwin, he seemed smaller. A colt-like boyishness, typical of a certain kind of young white American, was still as much a part of him as dew on early-morning grass. He was talking with Baldwin about a possible movie concerning an interracial romance, presumably with script by Baldwin and with him as the white half of the romance. It seemed to me that Baldwin was the established artist, the authority in the matter they were discussing, and Warren Beatty was still getting there, but Baldwin behaved as if the roles were reversed, agreeing too readily with Warren Beatty, laughing too heartily at his jokes. I wondered if he was merely being a good host or whether it reflected his tremendous keenness to establish himself in the movie business.

A jacket of Baldwin's latest book lay on a table; on the back was a photograph of Baldwin in the kind of clothes Brando usually wore in his movies. It was as though Baldwin had selected the most unliterary picture he could find of himself. I made some remark about Jimmy Baldwin as Marlon Brando and Warren Beatty laughed, and it annoyed me to see the young Hollywood actor, so green beside Baldwin, laughing at him, even though I was the cause of it. Baldwin, usually so good at facing up to things, didn't care for his own image; he didn't want to be seen as a literary figure. The jacket photo was only one of many attempts to run away from it—often he talked about himself in terms of jazz musicians or blues singers, the

152

kind of artists who meant something to young blacks in the Harlem streets. How hard to be a writer when the people you identified with most dug music rather than books—there was a tendency for many of them to think of books as the exclusive concern of white people, yet what a matter for pride it could be when someone from the Harlem streets beat whites at their own highfalutin game! Yet beyond this fantasizing, this role-playing, I wondered if the photograph also reflected the dreams of the little boy who had believed himself ugly because the world had told him he was so often. Had he often dreamed not of being a writer but of being handsome, muscular, athletic, filling out the kind of form-fitting clothes the slickest dudes on the street wore, the wardrobe of a Brando in the movies? How ironic if this feeling lay behind his overly respectful treatment of handsome young Warren Beatty.

I was reminded of this when I attended a party given by Baldwin's sister, Gloria, and her new husband from Africa, Frank Karefa-Smart, who was working at the United Nations. Most of the guests were merrily dancing, while Baldwin sat sedately in an armchair. "I feel like Henry James," he told me impatiently and joined the dancing enthusiastically, as if to show he was still a party type like the rest of the family and not a literary figure sitting on his dignity.

Mailer revealed a similar feeling when on the back of one of his book jackets he had reproduced a photograph of himself with a big black eye. He looked as if he had just left, not the typewriter like most authors, but the boxing ring. Unlike Baldwin, he wasn't trying to counter boyhood fears of ugliness, the insecurity of blackness, but he was giving that nice Jewish boy way back in the past a big black eye. He no more wanted to be a literary figure than Baldwin did; that was too restricting for the size of his ambitions. But as far as the great competitive world, in which they both lived, was concerned, their fears of ugliness or niceness/cowardice came to the same thing—a handicap in the game of winning and losing.

Neither the Brando nor the Warren Beatty movies was

made. Stokeley Carmichael never became a movie star; he went back down South where he was another kind of star. I played back my memories of Baldwin's smiling, uncritical reception of Brando and Beatty—had he been uncritical because he'd known how it would all turn out?

12

For many white Americans—including Norman Mailer, who needed an equalizer against black rivals like Baldwin—the Vietnam War came almost as a relief: here was a civil rights movement in which no black could pull rank!

However liberal whites felt about the black struggle, however much they agreed with its aims and even demonstrated side by side with blacks, most whites could not identify deeply because they were not personally involved, not on the receiving end themselves. Without direct experience, without the appeal of saving yourself as well as others, there was a limit to commitment.

But the Vietnam War was different—my God, if you didn't have to go off to fight it yourself, your son was in danger of being drafted, with a big chance of going to Vietnam and statistically a pretty good chance of getting wounded or even killed. It wasn't a matter only of liberal principles here, but of direct personal involvement and real potential danger; it was amazing what a difference that made.

Those most likely to be directly affected, the young, were the quickest to reject the war as a blind patriotic duty, but many older people, too old to fight, also took to the streets. White people, that is. The blacks on the whole tended to react as whites had toward their struggle—with an expression of agreement, of disgust, a principled stand, but with not much per-

155

sonal commitment. There was even a suspicion among some blacks that the war was being used to divert attention from their struggle at home. Whites criticized blacks for standing aside, much as blacks had criticized them a few years earlier. Many young blacks in the streets had traditionally chosen the army as the only career open to them, and so a large proportion of the Vietnam casualties were black, but this still did not make the blacks see opposition to Vietnam as a cause comparable to civil rights. In a subtle way, Vietnam remained a white cause, a white fight; killing Vietnamese seemed to many blacks merely an extension of white racism; and so they waited and watched while whites at home opposed each other over the war . . .

Mailer and Baldwin, as in so much else in the sixties, represented the essence of the two sides. Both were among the first to condemn the war, but whereas Mailer became directly involved—with none of the inhibitions he had showed in the cause of the black struggle—Baldwin obviously saw it as no new conflict but merely the latest natural growth of the racism he had been fighting all his life. He did not write or speak out against Vietnam with the same unrelenting passion as he had against the scene at home. Vietnam was a branch; he gave most of his attention to the roots.

But for Mailer it was a—the!—perfect example of so much he had already diagnosed; all his theories, his imaginative voyagings, were being proved in practice. The war came out of the plague; it was cancer rampant; the kind of mad act that happened when the two sides of man, of a country—of Lyndon Johnson!—were unbalanced. Could we at least hope that the country, like Rojack-Mailer in *An American Dream,* might be better for releasing the madness, or was it just a matter of passing on the plague to the rest of the world? Mailer was too much involved to look very far ahead. The growing resistance among whites had even brought all his White Negroes out of hiding—or imitation White Negroes; it was hard to tell the would-bes from the real thing as the white middle-class young showed their resistance to the war by their very dress, hair styles, and behavior. Drugs that had been the tools or play-

things of extremists, even when Mailer was a young writer not
too many years before, suddenly became as popular as liquor
in the days of prohibition, partly for reasons of protest or
escape from parents who still supported the war or whose ways
of life seemed to make it necessary. Vietnam provided plenty
of ammunition for the war between the generations that seemingly went on forever in America.

Mailer could look on these protesting young with an almost
parental air, for he had helped to invent them. Baldwin, too,
might take some ironic pleasure in their styles of resistance, for
much of their behavior and appearance imitated blacks (or
blacks as they saw them; much cruder versions of Mailer's
white negroes). In rebelling against their own way of life, they
had become much more sympathetic to, much more able to
identify with, the people whom their society made natural
rebels; the Establishment seemed to be getting at them, too,
now—they were safe to be comfortably liberal no longer! It was
a form of flattery, this imitation of and identification with
blacks, but it was flattery of the appearance rather than the
reality of black experience. Young blacks might be amused by
these white contemporaries of theirs, might be pleased, or pa-
tronizing, or contemptuous, depending on how well they con-
trolled their own resentments, anger, rage. But to older blacks
like Baldwin—he was becoming middle-aged now, like Mailer
—the white kids at least seemed promisingly open-minded.
Surely when they grew up and acquired some power they would
be more progressive than their parents, though there was always Robert Frost's warning about young radicals turning into
old conservatives to haunt any high hopes of greater understanding, of some genuine coming together.

Martin Luther King, who with his wife, Coretta, had been
an early opponent of the war—as his hero, Mahatma Gandhi,
had been of other wars—began to talk not only in terms of
freeing blacks but of liberating underprivileged whites, too—
of bringing together all the poor, black and white. From addressing at the most a smallish minority, no more than twenty
per cent of the population, King was suddenly thinking in

terms of a coalition that might add up to a possible majority. It was a thought that could give politicians in Washington, D.C., nightmares; many of them had been scared enough of the civil rights movement that had taken over the early sixties, but that could be kept in its place; this concept of King's was a much greater threat to the status quo. Many of King's white supporters from among the powerful—established blacks, too —who had felt safe with his message of nonviolence, turned against him when he spoke this way, but since resistance to Vietnam couldn't be silenced, whatever an increasingly despotic Lyndon Johnson did, King's new ideas began to catch fire.

Both Kennedy and Johnson were tough, established, pragmatic politicians, but Kennedy's style appealed to Mailer the romantic, whereas Johnson's did not. He had seen promise in Kennedy and the politician in him could identify with JFK; not for nothing had Rojack-Mailer once gone on a double date with JFK. But imagine a double date with LBJ! Johnson offended not only the romantic in Mailer but the realist, too. He was reminded of his army service in Texas. Along with an English accent, he loved to imitate a Texan, and as his former wife, Lady Jeanne, was his model for the English, LBJ was his model Texan: big, loud, devious, conniving, sometimes crude, with delusions of grandeur—the Emperor. Vietnam became a personal matter between Mailer and LBJ, and Mailer dedicated a collection of his latest pieces, including several Vietnam broadsides, "to Lyndon B. Johnson, whose name inspired young men to cheer for me in public." This was a reference to his sudden blossoming as a public speaker, a politician in the making, as pro as any other on the platforms of the country. He might not get cheers from hard hats or middle-class conservatives, but the students loved him when he told them the war was crazy, a part of the plague they should not help to spread.

Mailer went along with the idea that Vietnam was an attempt—LBJ's attempt—to divert the country, to absorb its energies. LBJ, according to Mailer, believed so much in Image that he thought what made the headlines was more real to people than the events themselves. It was not what Mailer called "the Negro Movement" that possessed the real importance, it was the movement's "ability to get space in the papers." The president felt, Mailer said, that he had no issue, no program, no slogan, "with which to slow down the Nigras and their Rights." The movement's ability to crowd everything else out of the newspapers meant that as far as he was concerned it was out of control. "There was going to be no way to control the Negro Movement, and no way to convince the Negro Movement that their victory was due to his particular attentions." (Did Mailer dislike LBJ so much because, if he had been president in his place, he might have had many of the same thoughts?) So, according to Mailer, LBJ needed another issue and Vietnam provided it. If there was one thing "hotter than Harlem in the summer," it was "air raids on rice paddies and napalm on red gooks." And when the war got too good, and everybody was giving too much space to that, he could always tell the Nigras—how Mailer relished that Texan accent!—that it was a good time to be marching on the White House; when they got a little too serious he could bring back Vietnam. "The President felt like the only stud in a whorehouse on a houseboat."

This was a lip-smacking theory Mailer presented in a speech at Berkeley—California was reputed to have more White Negroes that year than anyplace else—and he defended such fantasizing on the grounds that only in the irrational, the imaginative, the surrealistic, could you understand anything as irrational as America's involvement in Vietnam. The argument that it was another stage in a world struggle against communism didn't satisfy him, unless it was part of an overall fantasy that had us eventually destroying China's nuclear potential (though Mailer was naturally a little ambivalent about the idea of the U.S. versus communism because it appealed to the competitive side of him). You had to look for explanations, he said, not at the Kremlin or Peking but at the psyche of LBJ. He was "alienated from judgment," he was "close to an imbalance which at worst could tip the world from orbit." LBJ was a member of a real minority group; this did not mean being a member of a category—a Negro or a Jew—but being a man who felt his existence in a particular way, forced to live with two opposing notions of himself: he saw himself as both exceptional and insignificant, good and evil. The only way he might relieve the unendurable tension that surrounded any sense of his own identity was to define his nature by his own acts; to discover his courage or cowardice by actions that engaged his courage . . .

Was Mailer speaking only of LBJ, or of himself, too? "A Negro or a Texan, a President or a housewife, is by this definition a member of a minority group if he contained two opposed notions of himself at the same time . . ." One's emotions were forever locked in ambivalence; the expression of an emotion was forever releasing its opposite; the ego was in perpetual transit "from the tower to the dungeon and back again." He told the Berkeley crowd that by this definition, nearly everyone in America was a member of a minority group.

This was a thought that Martin Luther King was approaching, but Mailer's conclusion was very different. He saw such people, alienated from the self by a double sense of identity, at the mercy of a self that demanded action and more action to define the most rudimentary borders of identity. "It is a demand which will either kill a brave man or force him to grow, but when a coward is put in need of such action he tears the wings of flies . . ." The great fear was not that LBJ was close to insanity but that he expressed the near insanity of most of us, and his need for action was America's need for action—any kind of action "to get the motors going." And thus Mailer found his way back to his old theme: "A future death of the spirit lies close and heavy upon American life, a cancerous emptiness at the center which calls for a circus. The country is in disease . . ."

Mailer was addressing not only the Berkeley students but fellow whites in general. This became doubly clear if you compared what he was saying with Baldwin's writing at the same time. Both writers were clearly addressing their own race.

Whereas to Mailer LBJ was like a skeleton in the family closet, to Baldwin he was one of Them, a white in power, not a black's responsibility. Baldwin's attitude became increasingly aloof—"All of the Western nations have been caught in a lie, the lie of their pretended humanism . . ."—whereas Mailer always felt a sense of identification, even ending a letter to President-Elect Nixon with "Yours for an interesting and prosperous Administration."

Mailer the political theoretician, in fact, was thirsting for action; he had an LBJ-urge to get out there and press the flesh. Public speeches, more and more interviews that became like one-man press conferences—he was steadily leaving behind the sedentary, cerebral writer; here he was practically on the barricades. It all came together for Mailer in an invitation to take part in a March on Washington and an attempt to disrupt the Pentagon; it would be the next best thing to combat in Vietnam. At first, however, he was unwilling to go. The invitation came from an old friend he didn't associate with winning moves. And, as he admitted himself, he "hated to put in time with losers." For years, he said, he had had the reputation of being a loser and it had cost him much. But now he had at least reached the stage of winning a few and even when he lost, he did it with style (Boom! and baroque). So if he went to Washington and he was on the losing side—as it seemed he would be, because the Pentagon could summon a bigger army than they could—then he would do it in a Mailerian way. What that added up to was giving both sides of himself their freedom on stage. Mailer the voyeur-reporter would once more become an extremist-activist, or as much as he could be in his more conservative middle age. Once more he would challenge accepted, established ideas in his behavior and adventure out there way beyond secure lines. Like Joyce taking an epic approach to an ordinary day in Dublin, he intended to turn this Vietnam protest, one of so many, into a major confrontation of everything in American life.

Giving himself a leading role in reporting on the battle, he wrote objectively as "Norman Mailer." Yet streams of consciousness occasionally washed away the objective reporter altogether, and a few old grudges were paid off in some of the character sketches. Poor Paul Goodman! The author of *Growing Up Absurd* had an honorable record of trying to wake up students to the realities of life, and was as much of a hero on radical campuses as Mailer himself, but he had once called Mailer "a chump" in *Dissent,* the intellectual quarterly, and he had clearly not been forgiven. Goodman had written of Kennedy's "cool and activist role-playing of vitality in a situation of impotence"; Mailer, he said, had responded accurately to the type in calling it hipster, but he had missed its meaning. According to Mailer, writing in his historic war correspondent's third person, "Goodman was a sexologue—that is, an ideologue about sex—Mailer was then also a sexologue; no war so rich without quarter as the war between two sexologues." Mailer then went on to report that sexologue-Goodman had related the "wargasms" of the Kennedy administration to the existential and Reichian notions of the orgasm Mailer had discussed in *The White Negro.* Goodman's charge had been "something to the general effect that the false prophet of the orgasm was naturally attached to the false hero of Washington who went in for wargasms . . ."

New York literary life was full of these sour old memories—generally of some review no one else now remembered except the author—but few harbored grudges so long and aggressively, it seemed. Baldwin, for example, had no reason to feel friendly toward Paul Goodman, who had described *Another Country* as "mediocre" and "unworthy of its author's lovely abilities," but he made no big thing of it as Mailer did; he seemed to reserve his most bitter thrusts for fellow blacks, perhaps because they could betray him in a way he didn't feel whites could. That remark of Goodman's about Baldwin's "lovely abilities" recalled Mailer's old crack about Baldwin's perfumed style. Mailer had said much the same as Goodman about *Another Country,* finding much of it "abominably written" and adding that possibly Saul Bellow, who was white and Jewish, succeeded in his novel, *Henderson the Rain King,* "in telling us more about the depths of the black man's psyche" than Baldwin did. What a clever way of dealing with his insecurities about blacks—particularly a rival writer like Baldwin—to claim a Jewish writer who also worked as a professor could convey more of a black man's psyche than the leading black spokesman!

Mailer's account of his Washington experiences is curiously studded with plugs and backslapping that remind one of a politician making the rounds, squeezing the flesh in a literary version of LBJ. Whereas Goodman, who had much in common with Mailer, is put down, others who would seem to have nothing in common with a man of Mailer's temperament and beliefs are given his approval, or at least his approval wrung through his war-correspondent brand of irony, which sometimes ends by taking away more than was originally conceded. He also worries continually about being liked, as if he is counting the votes. It is a strange attitude for a man who at the same time allows himself wild, don't-care acts, some of them on stage.

Mailer's old critic, *Time* magazine, reported that Mailer was "mumbling and spewing obscenities as he staggered about the stage" while addressing a meeting in Washington. *Time* also quoted Mailer as saying, "I'm here because I'm like LBJ. He's as full of crap as I am." Read this way, his behavior as described by *Time* seemed like a parody of Texan-LBJ, or was it simply that LBJ and chameleon-Mailer now had much in common?

Mailer walked around Washington with an early copy of his new novel, *Why Are We in Vietnam?*. His chief character, D.J., is a young Texan who talks like a hipster son of LBJ's, Mailer's ideal Texan whose spirit was the cause of all our Vietnam troubles. Rojack-Mailer had made way for D.J.-Mailer, just as Kennedy was replaced by LBJ. Vietnam is mentioned only twice in the novel—on the last page—but the whole book is a fictional replay of Mailer's political speeches about LBJ's psyche and Vietnam.

When Mailer came to write his own account of the Washington affair, calling it *The Armies of the Night,* he began by quoting the *Time* report and commented: "Now we may leave *Time* in order to find out what happened." Mailer's account was certainly different, much more detailed as regards motive, but the role he played was basically the same—half inspired clown, a Shakespearean Fool, and half a combative Irishman, an aging Sergius O'Shaugnessy. As Mailer explained himself in *The Armies of the Night*, "the modest everyday fellow of his daily round was servant to a wild man in himself." This other side of "Norman Mailer," Mailer said, did not appear very often, but when it did, he was "an absolute egomaniac, a Beast." Was this a hint of how he felt now about that stabbing incident long ago? It was also a reminder of what he said about LBJ and membership in a minority group, "alienated from the self by a double sense of identity and so at the mercy of a self which demands action . . ." That now seemed to fit D.J.-Mailer as much as LBJ. And the "Beast"—the "self which demands action"—was to make one of its rare appearances while Mailer was in Washington, as he reported with relish.

Mailer, in fact, was in a very self-confident, LBJ mood when he wrote *The Armies of the Night;* he made a host of potentially damaging confessions with the relish that LBJ once displayed his operation scars. A party lacked flavor for him "unless someone very rich or social was present"—here was Mailer seeking the company of winners. One of the reasons he detested napalm in Vietnam was that he assumed its effect on the countryside was comparable to "the ravages of booze on the better foliage of his brain"; he often blamed some of his wilder actions years before on the ravages of booze or drugs. He hated being modest, he declared aggressively, "because modesty was an old family relative, he had been born to a modest family, had been a modest boy, a modest young man, and he hated that, he loved the pride and the arrogance and the confidence and the egocentricity he had acquired over the years . . ." He summed himself up: "Mailer was a Left Conservative." Or at other times he might have called himself a Right Revolutionary; he always described himself in terms of that "double sense of identity."

Mailer got his reward for going to Washington—he was ar-

164

rested and spent a few hours in jail—and he looked again into the eyes of the law, cops and courts, which seemed to bring out all his most conservative qualities, as if part of him had a politician's yearning for the law's power; it probably also awakened the fears of that former modest boy. And of course he couldn't resist once more giving the Mailer version of blacks.

One MP blocking the way was "a young Negro, part white," but Mailer found him disappointingly ordinary, not his idea of a Negro at all—he had "no Harlem smoke, no devil swish." Another young black, balanced daringly on the edge of a parapet, carried a placard, "No Vietnamese ever called me a nigger." That was more to Mailer's liking. He commented: "Was a mad genius buried in every Negro? How fantastic they were at their best—how dim at their worst . . ." But he found once more that blacks were not going to let whites star in any scene of theirs; those in Washington withdrew to hold their own demonstration, reluctant, as they put it, to use their bodies in a White War. As Mailer saw it, "If the Negroes were at the Pentagon and did not preempt the front rank, they would lose face as fighters; if they were too numerous on the line, they would be beaten half to death." That was the ostensible reason they didn't go, Mailer said, but he concluded that the real reason lay deeper—that the militant Negroes no longer wanted equality but demanded superiority. They felt superior and perhaps, Mailer was ready to admit, they were—a hard admission. But the proofs of superiority he found were still of a romantic, primitive kind that probably would still enrage Baldwin; the Black Negro was naturally superior to the White Negro . . .

In *The Armies of the Night,* I came across a quote from what I'd told Mailer about Snick—or SNCC, as Mailer called it more formally—when I'd tried to persuade him to go down South and write about the Freedom Riders. He referred to me as "an English journalist" who had once described the "panache" of SNCC, and he waxed on, as I had, about their cavalier style and plumage. Mailer's enthusiasm worried me; I didn't trust his romantic view of the black scene and I wondered if what appealed to him—the romantic extremism of Snick—was also what had appealed to me, and we both had missed the point.

When *The Armies of the Night* was published, Mailer's account of his struggle with the Establishment in Washington was twice blessed by the literary Establishment, for it was awarded both a Pulitzer Prize and a National Book Award. Respectability had come at last to the aging rebel; his long struggle back from the edge had been rewarded. Maybe it was time now to run for office—if not president, then his old dream of being mayor of New York, on an existential ticket, of course.

13

I met one of Mailer's former wives, the one he dedicated a book to as "Jeanne Louise Slugger Campbell." In *The Armies of the Night,* he had referred to this wife, his third, as a love affair with England, "and the fine dialectic of propriety and wickedness, manner and the mode of social murder in well-established places." I wasn't sure what that meant and so I was eager to meet the lady in question.

We had been reporters at the same time covering some of the same events, and we knew some of the same journalists in New York and London, so we met as fellow gossips, even though I had come with a proposition. I was working as a book editor at the time and I suggested that she write a book about an Anglo-American marriage, hers to Mailer. The idea appealed to her, so she went away to brood over it; I thought she'd mention it to Mailer and he'd kill it, but she suggested another meeting to talk some more about it. She had ambitions to be an actress and I suggested that she write a play about her grandfather, Lord Beaverbrook, with a fat part in it for herself. It was then she recalled her feeling that there was part of her in the murdered wife in *An American Dream.*

Baldwin's name came up, and she laughed and said she thought he made Norman nervous; she remembered one occasion when Baldwin was supposed to be calling with one of his sisters and Norman was very jumpy and made sure everything

167

was just right for the visit. In talking about the book, she had reminisced a little about the marriage—she and Norman had not been on speaking terms when they broke up and remained that way for about a year, but now they were good friends. But I never heard from her again. I supposed she had checked with Norman and he had been against it; his ex-wives probably all ended up friends with him, as loyal as Baldwin's brothers and sisters and friends were to him.

Baldwin and Tony Maynard, the old friend I had first met him with, had had some kind of falling out; something to do with their civil rights activities and as complicated as family rows generally are. I couldn't follow what it was about; when Maynard's name came up in the presence of the Baldwin family, it was as though shutters had come down with all except Mrs. Baldwin. Baldwin's mother had no blind loyalty to her children; if you had a quarrel with them, it was possible that they were in the wrong, and if she liked you, she would make up her own mind. When I thought about her, she always seemed to be a big strong woman, but in reality she was small and dainty, as slightly built as her famous son. She had many mannerisms that he had inherited and made well known, particularly some facial expressions and a quick rushing walk that had great charm. She had held together a large family of sturdy individualists, a very religious woman who never preached at you. She made sure her famous son ate regularly when he was home and tidied up around him and his occasionally wild friends, but otherwise she stayed in the background, like a human radiator warming the whole house. She still talked readily about Tony Maynard, but the rest of the family didn't. When I was in Harlem with David Baldwin once, we walked into Tony and a German girl friend coming out of Count Basie's, and Tony and David kept their distance like two gunmen not knowing whether or not they were in for a duel. "How's Jimmy?" Tony asked, and David shrugged. It was sad among good friends.

I attended a party which included some of Baldwin's African in-laws. I had met the whole gamut of African classes in England—from African sailors who had jumped ship in Liverpool and had hidden away in the ghetto in my hometown to the sons of prosperous Africans who were at college or finishing school in England or were learning some business. Often these well-to-do Africans seemed to have more in common with the rich English than with fellow Africans who had jumped ship. Most of the Africans you met in New York were rich, conservative people at home, but in America their color made them automatically radical, and they talked against the status quo in a way they would never have done at home, where they had more to lose now that they had taken over from the colonials.

Baldwin made a great fuss of his African in-laws and their friends. The African connection, the very idea of Africa, seemed to give him a feeling of security, and that day he appeared to need it. "When things go to hell here," he told me somberly, "I'll have somewhere to take my family." He was always worrying about his family—which included his growing number of nephews and nieces—but that day all his worries came to the surface and spoiled the party for him. Brock Peters, a black actor, was talking to him, but Baldwin seemed to be only half-listening. Peters was talking about a black show business celebrity who, he said, frequented the 42nd Street area and picked up young hustlers. He went on and on, very righteous in condemning the man, while Baldwin gloomily studied the floor—you couldn't tell where his head was. I said quietly that perhaps the celebrity had become bored with the company of fellow show business people and found some kind of release in the excitement of the streets; it might not even be some far-out sexual need, but simply a vacation from the tension of performance and the social role his famous name thrust upon him. Brock Peters surveyed me as if, since I was white, I couldn't possibly understand what he was talking about. Then, turning his broad back on me, he continued to address the silent Baldwin, who had not reacted at all but remained a detached, gloomy Hamlet. At last Peters paused, and then Baldwin spoke—quietly, moodily, almost to himself—but it was not about the celebrity on 42nd Street. He talked instead of the Black Panthers, and then I thought I knew what was troubling him so deeply.

The new black generation had gone even deeper into itself; Black Power interested it far more than any integration with whites; and the Black Panthers, with their uniforms and weapons and aggressive bravado, were a manifestation of all their feelings and yearning for independence, the latest stage in overcoming the years of brainwashing. Snick, once the most radical of the frontline groups, seemed staid and conservative in comparison. The Black Panthers scared most whites as much as the Black Muslims did, and the FBI and local police forces began to follow them around and harass them. The Panthers accepted the challenge and, instead of making way as was customary for survival in the ghetto, stood their ground, whatever the consequences. Such confrontations could only end violently, and Baldwin, who identified so closely with the black young, was worrying over what he could do to help.

Far from being an illegal and lawless organization, as they were treated, the Panthers, Baldwin believed, were a great force for peace and stability in the ghetto as long as they weren't forced like rats into a corner. But you couldn't expect white people to understand that, he said in a tone of great contempt. "With abject cowardice," the people in the Northern cities were allowing the Panthers to be threatened, jailed, even murdered. He said that, given the present conditions and the natural impatience of the new generation who thought blacks had waited long enough for their rights, the emergence of the Panthers' leader, the youthful Huey Newton, was as inevitable as the stand of Rosa Park years before, when she had refused to give her seat to a white man on a Montgomery, Alabama, bus.

Baldwin was in such a gloomy mood about the treatment of the Panthers that I caught some of the backwash. Leaving his African in-laws, he suddenly turned very dramatic about the chances of getting a cab in the streets; none of them might stop for a black man like him, he told the Africans. And he asked me if I'd go down with my white face and stop one and then

170

he'd come and get in it. The Africans seemed slightly puzzled; they couldn't understand why he didn't do it the rich way and tell the doorman downstairs—who was white anyway—to get a cab. I was irritated because I didn't want to play the White Man in some little scene Baldwin was staging for his African in-laws, whom I didn't know but who were obviously in the ruling class in their own country. But, understanding that Baldwin was under intense inner pressure and that this was some kind of release, I went downstairs and played my role. I remembered what he'd told me not long after the occasion of Tony Godwin's Chinese intervention: "Please don't mind or be embarrassed by any of my more hysterical outbursts. I'm like that on the top sometimes, but I'm very sound at bottom."

What a shock it must have been to Baldwin when the Panthers' laureate, the Minister of Information for the Black Panther Party for Self-Defense, attacked him and praised—of all people—Norman Mailer! Eldridge Cleaver, who described himself as an Afro-American born in Little Rock, Arkansas, praised Mailer's *The White Negro* as "prophetic and penetrating in its understanding of the psychology involved in the accelerating confrontation of black and white in America." Furthermore, Cleaver said he was personally insulted by Baldwin's "flippant, schoolmarmish dismissal" of it. He said (in his book *Soul on Ice,* which became a big best-seller, particularly among young whites) that Mailer had described the first important chinks in the "mountain of white supremacy," the desperate attempt of a new generation of white Americans to escape from the big white lies that compose the monolithic myth of White Supremacy/Black Inferiority and to enter into the cosmopolitan egalitarian spirit of the twentieth century. On the other hand, he found in Baldwin's work "the most grueling, agonizing, total hatred of the blacks, particularly of himself, and the most shameful, fanatical, fawning, sycophantic love of the whites that one can find in the writings of any black American writer of note in our time."

Having come up with this thesis—which must have astonished whites who were still nursing the wounds inflicted by

171

Baldwin's vigorous attacks on them—Eldridge Cleaver forced everything in Baldwin's work to prove his point. This approach was a politician's, not a writer's. The Minister of Information was using Baldwin to put over a message just as much as the Soviet politicians used Pasternak and Solzhenitsyn as whipping boys. What Cleaver was concerned about apparently was the black image, rather than the truth of the black experience, good and bad. Much of what Baldwin wrote was not good for the image; therefore he must hate blacks—it couldn't be that he respected and loved them enough to think they could survive even the truth. Cleaver went back to the early Baldwin essays, some of them written twenty years before, and with a politician's carefree way of quoting out of context, set about proving his point. He praised qualities in Baldwin's work at the same time he was condemning it, no doubt lest his audience might think he was being unfair—he was, but he mustn't appear so. He concluded that there was a decisive quirk in Baldwin's vision "which corresponds to his relationship to black people and to masculinity." It was this same quirk, Cleaver claimed, that compelled Baldwin to slander the character of Rufus Scott, the young black who commits suicide in *Another Country* (Rufus, in fact, was drawn with great love); venerate André Gide (Cleaver should have read Baldwin more carefully); repudiate *The White Negro* (for reasons Cleaver doesn't face); and drive the blade of Brutus into the corpse of Richard Wright (this is corny political rhetoric that wouldn't even go over well at a political party convention). Between the lines of *Soul on Ice,* of course, Cleaver showed his hand. He revealed a male chauvinist's attitude toward women, toward heterosexuality and homosexuality. He closely related sex and violence, and confused nonviolence with what was weak, and, to him, womanish. Baldwin—this summarized the charges against him—embodied in his art "the self-flagellating policy of Martin Luther King."

The Minister of Information didn't succeed in proving his case against Baldwin, not even by making use of the very early work in which Baldwin confessed to a good deal of self-hatred and therefore hatred of being black, and toward the end of his onslaught Cleaver became progressively wilder. Baldwin despised Richard Wright's masculinity: "He cannot confront the stud in others—except that he must either submit to it or destroy it . . ." But what Cleaver did succeed in doing was to point out chinks in the armor of the Panthers. Their view of life, as laid down by Cleaver, contained the same machismo, winners-and-losers, survival-of-the-fittest attitude they condemned in the society they were struggling against. Many of their beliefs—and their ways of expressing them—seemed as narrow and intolerant as those of white racists. And if you accepted Cleaver's interpretation, his approval of Mailer seemed merely to reveal Mailer's own ambivalent attitude toward the society he saw as plague-ridden. I wondered whether Mailer, any more than Baldwin, would see himself in Cleaver's picture of them, encountering each other in the eye of a social storm, traveling in opposite directions—"the white boy, with knowledge of white Negroes, was traveling toward a confrontation with the black, with Africa; while the black boy, with a white mind, was on his way to Europe . . ."

Baldwin took his time about replying, and when he did, he turned the other cheek in a way Martin Luther King might have approved of. He said that when he first met Cleaver in California with Huey Newton, he had been very much impressed, but he sensed a certain constraint between them: "I felt that he didn't like me—or not exactly that: that he considered me a rather doubtful quantity." What it probably meant, however, was that Cleaver was apprehensive over Baldwin's reception of what he'd written about him, but Baldwin hadn't then read it. By the time he had, Cleaver had gone into exile abroad, on the run from the police, and so it was probably Baldwin's turn to feel constraint.

Naturally, he wrote in *No Name in the Street,* he hadn't liked what Cleaver had had to say about him "at all." But he had admired *Soul on Ice* as a whole and thought he could see why Cleaver had felt compelled to issue what was, in fact, a warning. "He seemed to feel that I was a dangerously odd,

173

badly twisted, and fragile reed, of too much use to the Establishment to be trusted by blacks." Baldwin said sternly he felt Cleaver used "my public reputation" against him both naively and unjustly, "and I also felt that I was confused in his mind with the unutterable debasement of the male—with all those faggots, punks, and sissies, the sight and sound of whom, in prison, must have made him vomit more than once . . ." Baldwin here seemed to be playing a machismo role himself, spiking Cleaver's guns, for the "faggots, punks, and sissies" had a point of view of their own, and probably took a dim view of a self-confessed rapist—the supreme male chauvinist—like Cleaver. "Well," Baldwin went on, "I certainly hope I know more about myself, and the intention of my work than that, but I *am* an odd quantity. So is Eldridge; so are we all . . ."

Artists and revolutionaries, he warned Cleaver, are both odd and disreputable, but seldom in the same way; they were both driven by a vision and needed each other "and have much to learn from each other." With the utmost politeness, careful to give no comfort to Cleaver's enemies, he warned Cleaver of the bad habits of politicians (which Cleaver had displayed in his essay in *Soul on Ice*), of not respecting the individual, and of assuming they knew better what the people wanted than the people themselves. Baldwin then went on to affirm his backing of the Panthers—alive, dead, active, in jail, or in exile. Beside Cleaver's self-serving rhetoric, Baldwin's was a masterly performance. I wondered what Mailer made of the exchange. Who was closer to his ideal of the superior Negro: Cleaver, who competed on his ground (it wasn't hard to imagine Cleaver and Mailer hand wrestling or putting on the gloves for a little sparring) or the more elusive Baldwin?

Or Muhammad Ali? The new heavyweight champion of the world, with his enthusiastic endorsement of his own good looks ("I'm the Prettiest"), mocked the machismo values of the boxing world—and of Mailer and Cleaver. A boxer was supposed to be a male warrior personified; call him "pretty," enthuse about his good looks as you might a woman's, and you were breaking all the rules, the sporting code (there was nothing

American sports fans fled from faster than the sexual symbolism of sports), and you were asking for trouble. A boxer was once killed in the ring after he'd suggested at the weigh-in that his opponent was effeminate and homosexual. Yet here was Muhammad Ali, the former Cassius Clay, telling everybody who would listen what a beautiful hunk of man he was and reciting effeminate stuff like poetry in praise of his own beauty. Yet nobody could raise a word against him, for he beat every tough, machismo, rule-keeping, code-following boxer he faced. How could you be both Narcissus and unbeatable Champ? Muhammad Ali, by such behavior, threatened the values of whole lifetimes much more than the Black Muslims or the Panthers or Martin Luther King ever did.

I once watched Ali on television in a bar near Madison Square Garden that was crowded with some of his oldest enemies, the white working class—postal delivery men, truck drivers, and other boxing fans—who resented Ali's refusal to play the traditional role of black boxer (a touch of primitive, of respectful Uncle Tom, of I've-got-rhythm). Even as a young boxer in the Olympic Games, Ali had rejected such stereotyping, and had instead displayed the kind of freedom usually associated only with artists. In that bar, they longed for him to be defeated.

It seemed a natural extension of his challenge to such values that he refused to be inducted into the army, and thus he became, after Martin Luther King, the most formidable black opponent of the Vietnam war. As a young boxer, Ali had lost a lot of his popularity when he changed his name and joined the scary Black Muslims. He based his refusal to serve in the army on the fact that he was a Muslim minister. If the Muslims had had the respectable Establishment recognition of the Catholics or the Baptists, he might have had no trouble, but the Muslims at that time were regarded more as a dangerous political group than a religion and he was not heard sympathetically. He was eventually stripped of his World Heavyweight title— it was the only way he could lose it apparently, since no one seemed able to beat him—and he also lost, at a conservative

175

estimate, several million dollars in future fights. The irony was that if he had gone along with the program, he would have had a very easy time in the army, giving exhibitions, helping recruitment, and being allowed home for big fights. It was also ironic that the official boxing world, which embraced any number of gangsters and crooked promoters and gamblers, had turned puritanically "patriotic" in Ali's case and gone along with the political attempt to punish him. *The* sport of machismo had shown itself to be very chicken when challenged by more powerful authority. But Ali, a mere individual, was true to himself, wouldn't concede to the combined might of official boxing and the army and worked-up public opinion, and he became a hero to black kids in a way that not even Joe Louis was, and a hero, too, to White Negroes and their imitations on campus. I once saw Ali's car come out of Madison Square Garden after the Supreme Court had ruled in Ali's favor and he was allowed to fight again, and his car was immediately surrounded by a huge crowd of small boys. The car couldn't move for a long time as the kids peered in the windows and climbed up the sides like monkeys to get a closer look at their hero. They were responding to Ali's nonconformist appeal to their youthful imaginations; to the artist for whom a boxing match was not just a physical encounter but a creative, cultural event—an occasion for educating the public.

How did Mailer respond to this challenge? By reading Ali not as a boxer so much as a black. Ali became the supreme example of all that Mailer had been saying since *The White Negro*. Boxers' training camps had to produce an ego able to bear huge pain and administer drastic punishment. Ali's ego—America's greatest ego!—was like the flow of a river of constant energy fed by a hundred tributaries of black love and the love of the white left. Ali went into the ring, after three years of exile, in his great comeback fight for the championship against Joe Frazier as "the mightiest victim of injustice in America." He was also—for Mailer's twentieth century, he admitted, was nothing if not a tangle of opposition—"the mightiest narcissist in the land." Mailer went through the supporters Ali had won to his side; it was an interracial group to gladden the heart of Martin Luther King. "Every beard, dropout, homosexual, junkie, freak, swinger, and plain simple individualist adored him. Every pedantic liberal soul who had once loved Patterson now paid homage to Ali. The mightiest of the Black psyches and the most filigreed of the white psyches were ready to roar him home, as well as every family-loving hardworking square American who genuinely hated the war in Vietnam . . ."

What, though, of Ali's mocking those machismo values? Well, at the end of his description of the great fight, Mailer writes about how Ali survived the last round of this "heathen holocaust" in some last exercise of the will, "some iron fundament of the ego not to be knocked out," and it was then "as if the spirit of Harlem finally spoke and came to rescue and the ghosts of the dead in Vietnam, something held him up," and he was still standing at the end. For all his ridiculing of machismo, his open praise of his own good looks, Ali "had shown America what we all had hoped was secretly true." And Mailer left no doubt what that was. "He was a man." As smartly as Baldwin had dealt with Cleaver, Mailer had turned Ali inside out and made him proof of the Mailer values. It was hard for anyone to deal with a philosopher so versatile, an opponent so wily. Was Mailer getting into training for a contest with Baldwin— for surely it had to come—a confrontation between the two of them, if not in Madison Square Garden, like Ali and Frazier, then in the arena of television?

Baldwin also enjoyed Ali's performance, but in a different way. Baldwin had never been happy with the old machismo kind of boxers, even when they were black, but Ali's game, his mockeries, his irony, his humor, his outwitting of the people who ran the boxing business, belonged to a style Baldwin had lived with all his life. Ali's triumphant openness was as much a victory for black values as opening up segregated lunch counters years ago.

But Baldwin had much more on his mind. The civil rights movement had reached a crossroads; the Panthers had lost a series of violent confrontations and were riddled with informers; the pendulum of black feeling began to swing back toward Martin Luther King and nonviolence, but the bigger King looked, the more *his* life was in danger. And, on a more private, personal level, Tony Maynard was in trouble, big trouble. He was accused of killing a Marine in the Village and had been extradited from Germany to stand trial.

Tony Maynard had great pride and dignity, and I could see him fighting if he was pushed, particularly if he thought the opponent was worthy of him, but murdering someone in the seedy early-morning circumstances described in the charge didn't sound like him at all. Baldwin said he didn't doubt Maynard's innocence either. Their serious disagreement, he told me, had been over the strategy needed to handle a rent strike and was now forgotten and forgiven; he'd do all he could to help. Since Maynard had some other influential friends, he should have been able to get a good lawyer, though in the end apparently Baldwin and Maynard's sister, Valerie, a talented sculptress, had to do most of the organizing of Maynard's defense. I wrote to him, offering to help in any way I could, but I didn't hear back. Baldwin said he was depressed, and that might explain it; he described how he'd gone over to see Maynard in prison in Hamburg before he was sent home. "I wanted to find out not only what I could do, but what mood, what condition, Tony was in, what was left in him for the fight. Sometimes, if the misfortune is so great and help arrives too late, you turn your face to the wall and then nobody can help you—it's too late. But the fight was still in Tony and, thank God, he didn't know how long a fight he had ahead of him."

American justice takes its time, often an interminable time, and it also takes your time, too, though, unlike the lawyers, you're not getting paid for yours. If Tony Maynard was found not guilty, nobody would be able to give him back the part of his life he'd spent proving it. Eventually the labyrinthine case reached court; the evidence seemed weak to me; but it ended in a hung jury, which meant Maynard would have to go through it all again. The next time, he was sent to prison, officially guilty, but there were still weak links in the evidence.

The more you examined them, the weaker they got, and in time
—oh, how much time!—Maynard and his lawyer were back in
court trying to convince a judge that they should go to trial
again. In theory, at least, until you're found guilty you're innocent, but once you've been found guilty then your whole position changes and you have few rights left. Another trial would
be expensive; getting it would be hard, uphill work.

The seedy courthouse (wherever our tax money was spent,
it certainly wasn't on our court buildings) reminded me of my
years as a police-court reporter in England. I had forgotten
how much depends on memory, the most unreliable part of
human equipment. In Tony Maynard's case, the memories of
policemen and other witnesses, whose evidence was under fire,
had to go way back into the past. Policemen kept saying "to
the best of my recollection," and the other witnesses said the
same in similar formal phrases. Nobody seemed to have any
notes they could refer to—not that notes written even immediately after an event are always reliable, for very few people can
remember accurately, but at least professionals should produce
such aids when a man's freedom is at stake. Policemen, in my
experience, have a tin ear for dialogue, and when I covered
courts regularly I kept a collection of the cleaned-up formal
speech they put into people's mouths. It always seemed strange
that defendants and witnesses never denied speaking that way.
Perhaps they were flattered or had agreed to the official version
beforehand. I was surprised that Tony Maynard's lawyer didn't
make more of the absence of police notes, but a lot is taken for
granted in such courts: it is like a game played according to
certain rigid rules accepted by both sides. The judge and the
district attorney's man often engaged in arguments, and I wondered why the judge allowed such heated repartee. His remark
later on that he had once been an assistant D.A. himself perhaps explained his lenience: judges have to come from somewhere, but they are the victims of their experience, too.

During one break, I talked over a wooden partition with
Tony Maynard. He had an ashy indoor complexion and the
closed expression of a prisoner, but otherwise he seemed in

179

good shape considering what he'd been through; there was no hint of the anger or the bitterness he must have felt. He seemed curiously serene—perhaps he was playing a role to impress the court in his favor, or maybe his experiences had been so bad that he had the serenity of someone who realizes that nothing worse can ever happen to him. He had been badly beaten up in the German prison; he had been nearly killed in a riot in an American prison. He must have wondered more than once if he would survive long enough to get his freedom.

We talked as if the new trial—and freedom—were only a matter of time now. More time. I asked him what his plans were when he got out. He replied with a grin—the kind of sneaky grin prisoners give one another—that his skin hadn't felt the sun for years, and he'd just like to lie on a beach. It was an embarrassing talk for me; unspoken between us was the feeling of how lucky I was to be free to go out whenever I wanted, whereas he would soon be on his way back to his cell. I could imagine how Baldwin must feel. The endless saga of getting Tony Maynard out of prison would seem to be the epitome of what blacks could expect from white justice, even then, even after all the events of the sixties. Baldwin would identify completely. I compared his feeling with Mailer's when he went to court. To Mailer, as to most whites, it would be an individual experience in a way it couldn't be to Baldwin.

I tried to imagine the world as Tony Maynard would see it when he came out again. It would be far less hopeful than when he went in. The great division was still there and yawning wider. Lyndon Johnson, the leader of the Vietnam war, and Martin Luther King, the leader of the civil rights movement, had rejected each other. LBJ had set the hounds of the FBI on King, and King was speaking out across the country against LBJ and our involvement in Vietnam. No confrontation, no dialogue, was possible between them, though it was very much needed. Was it possible that Baldwin and Mailer as advance patrols could stand in for them?

180

14

I finally did witness a meeting between them—a confrontation existential style.

It was at the home of Baldwin's publisher at that time, Richard Baron, and there were no television cameras, no newspaper photographers, just a select audience obviously expecting fireworks. Aquarius—as Mailer had taken to calling himself —versus Leo.

Mailer and several other white writers, including Philip Roth, James Jones, and William Styron, had just received huge, well-publicized advances, and Baldwin was said to be feeling left out and furious. The white boys were being treated better than he was! It didn't sound like Baldwin unless he was using the situation in negotiating a new contract with his publisher. In an apparent effort to placate him, his publisher had laid on a limousine to run him around the city and had invited him to a dinner party to which he could bring his own guests. Were the white boys treated any better than that?

Baldwin was in a strange, high-strung mood that night as he waited for the limousine to collect him and his guests at his apartment. He was drinking Johnny Walker Red quickly, nervously, and grinning broadly at any feeble joke. He reminded me of Muhammad Ali's near hysteria before the first fight with Sonny Liston (and, I reminded myself, Ali won that one). I had heard that Mailer was to be at the dinner party, and I wondered what kind of trouble Baldwin might be anticipating.

Baldwin's brother David, always a calming influence, sat beside him, solid, dependable, like his manager. Nat Hentoff, the political journalist, was there, looking like a sporty professor, the kind you might see at a big fight; perhaps he sniffed something for his column. Members of Baldwin's family drifted in and drifted out. His mother took a look at the rate he was consuming Scotch, sighed, but didn't say anything; he suddenly held her by the waist and kissed her, as if drawing strength from her. This was the way the high-spirited Ali had behaved with his entourage before he faced Liston—and beat him.

And suddenly we were on our way, Baldwin somber and calm now in the back seat of the limousine. Our destination was out of the city and we stopped at a high, dark apartment block to pick up Jules Feiffer, the political cartoonist and playwright, a tall, thin man with a poker-face who reminded me of William Burroughs. According to Mailer in *The Armies of the Night,* Feiffer had walked out of the National Book Award's assembly in protest against the Vietnam war—Vice-President Humphrey was about to speak—and "then sneaked back to go to a party for Humphrey." Mailer commented aggressively: "Feiffer's comet had not been in ascendance since." It was a mean crack; was Mailer paying off an old grudge? Perhaps if Mailer and Baldwin didn't provide the main bout of the evening, Mailer and Feiffer would.

The host and hostess came out to greet Baldwin; they fussed around him, laughing—they seemed very nervous. What were they expecting? David Baldwin had hurriedly followed his brother out of the limousine and never left his side; I was reminded of the way the Secret Service guarded the president. They all walked into the house, talking; I could hear Baldwin's quick, intense tones and his laughter. Then suddenly another voice cut across, a familiar, wary voice, often heard imitating the English, but tonight sounding more like a Brooklyn Dodger.

"Hello, Jimmy."

It was Mailer, looking stockier, his hair beginning to gray, but not carrying much fat. He had certainly slimmed down since the last time I'd seen him; he must have been in heavy training to get down to fighting weight. He stood flexing his shoulders, a half-grin on his face. I didn't like the look of that grin, and maybe our host and hostess didn't either—they stood there very uncertainly.

Baldwin and Mailer stared at each other—it was surprising how small they both were. Baldwin was so slight that a strong wind might have doubled him up, never mind a powerful punch, and Mailer, for all his greater weight was no taller and still looked vulnerable in the stomach. They went on and on staring, not speaking; the atmosphere was electric with tension. Then suddenly David Baldwin stepped between them, smiling, holding out his hand for Mailer to shake. He looked big and healthy, a formidable opponent. That broke the tension. Mailer's grin widened and he gripped David's hand, hunching his shoulders as if he was in the ring; then he and Baldwin exchanged careful handshakes and pats on the shoulders, but instead of talking together, catching up with each other's news like old friends, they quickly separated and disappeared inside their respective groups on opposite sides of the large living room—like two Napoleons surrounded by their marshals.

Mailer, too, had brought his own group with him—his fourth wife, Beverly (to whom he'd dedicated *The Armies of the Night*), and the oldest of his daughters, now of college age, and perhaps others; the room suddenly seemed full of people. I felt a little sorry for our host and hostess as they stood looking apprehensively from Baldwin's group to Mailer's, probably wondering if pre-dinner drinks would blend the groups and make them more friendly or send up the temperature and render them more hostile.

Baldwin, his teeth flashing in the phoney show business grin of Louis Armstrong, gave the appearance of being entirely at his ease. He and brother David indulged in a little subtle horseplay between them, with many slapped palms and other black gestures that might awaken a White Negro's envy in the watching Mailer. It all reminded me again of Muhammad Ali—this

183

time of Ali's trick of striding about the ring before a fight began, making outrageous, boastful jokes, psyching his opponent. But Mailer, as an old fight man, the new Hemingway and student of Ali, would be wary of such tricks. He would have his own tricks up his sleeve. He had given strong psychic powers to mere looks in *An American Dream,* and, in *The Armies of the Night,* when an MP's club had failed to land, he'd wondered if he now possessed "a moral force which implanted terror in the arms of young soldiers." I saw him shooting Baldwin plenty of long looks across the room, but they had no obvious effect; Baldwin either ignored them or warded them off with his own psychic powers.

The old competitive Mailer couldn't take this long-range engagement for long if it was to have no effect; perhaps he was even fearful of the long-term effect of the Baldwins' psyching operation. At any rate, he suddenly left the security of his group and ambled, shoulders square, chest like the traditional barrel, across the room to enter the rival group. People fell back to let him in.

Mailer faced Baldwin again, almost eyeball-to-eyeball; David stood beside his brother uncertainly, not knowing if he could interfere in a one-on-one confrontation, and yet obviously keen to take on Mailer himself. I saw the host and hostess watching helplessly—anything might happen. There must have flashed through all minds there what Baldwin and Mailer had said about each other over the years—this was another "Black Boy Looks at the White Boy" situation. Baldwin had said of that first encounter ages ago: "We were trapped in our roles and our attitudes: the toughest kid on the block was meeting the toughest kid on the block." They were still trapped in their roles and their attitudes, but the roles and attitudes were different now. They were spokesmen, celebrities, super-stars in a society that preached competition from the cradle to the grave. They were both recognized winners, and yet this would be forever between them: to Baldwin, they hadn't started equal; Mailer had had the inestimable advantage of being white in a white society, whereas Baldwin had started with the great

184

handicap of being black, one of the official losers. It must have infuriated Baldwin when he was young that he had so far to go before he even reached the starting place of people like Mailer. But now they were even, equal, how it must infuriate Mailer that he could never have a sense of victory, he could never *win;* he would always have a guilty feeling that he hadn't had to come as far as Baldwin. So Baldwin now could forgive him his advantageous start much more easily than he could ever accept it. For a man as competitive as Mailer always seemed to be— the man who admitted he didn't even like the company of "losers"—it must have been completely frustrating to face a literary rival and know that there was no way in which he could come out the winner.

Frustration can lead to a feeling of impotence, and that is when wild things can happen, as the host and hostess clearly recognized. But Baldwin, luckily, was still in his Ali mood and, with his brilliant Louis Armstrong smile—the White Negro wouldn't miss the meaning of that deadly front—he began to introduce people to Mailer, almost as if he was the host himself and Mailer was an unknown guest who didn't know anyone. This was a psyching move worthy of Ali himself, for without being immediately unpleasant—and he was too shrewd a player to confess defeat like that—there was little Mailer could do but go along with Baldwin, at least for the time being.

I was hoping that Baldwin would overlook me, that I could stay in the background, but he began to introduce me. Mailer, with his half-grin—the kind a boxer gives when he is hoping to lull his opponent into falling for a sucker punch—allowed that he knew me. Baldwin didn't then let it drop, unfortunately; he said something flattering about a book I'd written, dealing with my white-black experiences in the South, and Mailer allowed that he'd read it. Baldwin still didn't let me drop back into comfortable obscurity, that secure feeling of being outside the ring where the fight would take place, but said something about its being a good book for a white man to have written. Baldwin in fact had selected it as one of the three best books of that year, along with two books by black writers—a fact Mailer no doubt was aware of, because a sparrow hardly fell off a tree in the literary world without his knowing about it; such knowledge was part of being a good competitor. Baldwin doubtless had exaggerated the book's merits because my viewpoint was acceptable to him and because I had had some experiences across the lines ("You are not an exotic like me; you are a traitor," he had told me with some pleasure. "My point of view can be justified—and dismissed—by my color. Your color makes your point of view invalid"). Mailer himself had published a better book that year, but its viewpoint was less sympathetic, more competitive, from the other side of the lines; Baldwin was hardly likely to decorate a rival who kept to his privileged place. But I didn't feel that Baldwin was exaggerating my book's merits that night just to commend its interracial qualities or to make me feel good—in fact, he made me feel more uneasy. I assumed he was continuing to psych Mailer by playing white off against white, with me as nothing more than a pawn in the game. He repeated that it had been a good book for a white man to have written and he looked Mailer in the eye as he said it. Mailer had the choice of seizing on that "white man" crack or of ignoring it. He chose to ignore it, although it must have sorely strained his ego to do so. The alternative was to pick up the gauntlet and fight on Baldwin's terms, on Baldwin's ground. If he challenged that particular "white man" crack, he might fall for a thousand ambushes or booby traps before he made it back to some ground on which they could fight as equals. Mailer was too shrewd to fall for that; he didn't respond, and Baldwin, his gauntlet lying there ignored, could do nothing more than complete the introductions. So far so good.

The watching host and hostess seemed to let out a sigh of relief; their problem now was how to handle the situation when everybody sat down to eat. Most dinner parties have seating problems of one sort or another, arising out of everything from status to the anticipation of trouble. If these two formidable opponents were seated anywhere near one another, with the liquor flowing, were they likely to draw out old animosities like stilettos, turning the table into an uproar?

Taking the safest way out, the host and hostess split the dinner party into two, seating Mailer at one table and Baldwin at another, with the tables separate enough so that there would be no exchanges between them. I wondered how they would accept the arrangement; Mailer, in particular, might feel as though he was being treated patronizingly as an *enfant terrible* who couldn't be relied on to behave properly. But both Baldwin and Mailer merely took their places, meekly enough, at their respective tables.

Seated at Mailer's table, I was apprehensive that he, feeling frustrated, might treat me as a Baldwin stand-in or try to take it out of me for being a Baldwin pawn—or even "a traitor." But apart from some cracks about the English and the inevitable imitation of an English accent over the hors d'oeuvres, he left me alone to be a spectator in an exchange he had with David Baldwin. If Baldwin had a stand-in at that table, it was David, and he was an obvious challenge to Mailer. They began to joke with each other, a game that could easily escalate into something more serious once one gained the upper hand. But outwitting David at that game, especially if you were white, was like trying to get a grip on the oiled skin of a wrestler. Mailer's boxing spirit was matched against David Baldwin's uptown, streetwise, mental kung fu; it was a duel of wits that in the end was bound to make the more aggressive feel powerless.

Mailer was seated at one end of the table; his wife, Beverly, at the other. She had occasionally taken David Baldwin's side, and now Mailer, tiring of his frustrating exchanges with David, turned to spar with his wife. She was a tall, outgoing, articulate woman; an actress and, she'd told me over dinner, a former waitress in the South. She had also known Hemingway—that link again! When she began to exchange jokes and to argue with her husband up and down the table, she showed a smart waitress's talent for repartee, giving about as good as she got. Mailer was subtler and more crushing in debate, but she was faster and more pointed; he was more the aggressor, she the quick counter-puncher. Mailer had discussed his wives in *The*

Armies of the Night—"some part of four cultures" had been his through his four very different wives. He had said Beverly was "just as difficult as the rest, or more difficult—for he understood her the least." There were times, he added, "listening to her first-sergeant's tones in the middle of a quarrel when he had to dare a stroke in order to keep himself from beating up on her beautiful white Southern girl face." Her first-sergeant's tones were occasionally heard at that dinner party, and I wondered if in the end she would have to put up with her husband's angry frustration from spending the evening with a group of blacks, with the baddest black of them all, the arch rival, who had aces Mailer could never trump, whatever hand he gave himself.

But the dinner ended with no further trouble; the groups even continued to fraternize when they left their separate tables. Baldwin was talking with Beverly Mailer; the host and hostess were probably counting the minutes to departure time, but on the surface all was relaxed smiles now that the climax of the evening, the actual dinner, had been safely got through.

Everyone, as if weary from the tension in the house, decided to have an early night, and no one was urged to stay. I have never seen two more relieved, happier-looking people than our host and hostess as we began to put on our coats and get ready to leave. As the Baldwin group waited at the door for the limousine, Mailer suddenly left his group and came over. People tensed again—was some last-minute conflict still possible? David Baldwin turned from the door, smiling warily. Only Baldwin himself seemed calm and cool, back in his Ali mood after loosening up at the dinner table. But Mailer by-passed him and came over to me. "Your book," he said belligerently, "wasn't altogether right. It didn't jell." And he glanced at Baldwin. He'd tossed his gauntlet on the floor; a book Baldwin had praised to him he was now putting down. It was a devious way of getting at Baldwin; why not come at him head on? Was he still haunted by that "Negro irony" which, he had pointed out in *The Armies of the Night,* "could separate the most weathered hide from the most determined flesh—the wisdoms

188

of torture were in their skill"? At the table, he had playfully risked that "Negro irony" with David Baldwin; perhaps his lack of success had made big brother Jimmy Baldwin loom ever larger than life—what savage slash of "Negro irony" might the author of *The Fire Next Time* be capable of if he was sufficiently roused by a white opponent! Was Aquarius doomed forever to play a White Negro, second best, in any real, gutsy, deep-down, drag-out confrontation with his peer, Baldwin the Leo?

At any rate, Baldwin responded to Mailer's challenge the way Mailer had responded to his before dinner—by ignoring it. It was now too late for exercises of "Negro irony" and my English irony was no match. I didn't really care what Mailer thought of my book. I no longer had any interest in it; I'd written it because I'd believed what Somerset Maugham said —that you can free yourself from memories by writing about them—and I'd found it wasn't true, at least for me. So the book now was just a reminder I didn't want, but trying to tell Mailer that would have been like trying to convince someone you didn't love your own child. He'd have thought I was chickening out before his belligerence; I had to play his game, though English irony from me could be no match for the threat of Negro irony posed by Baldwin.

"I'm sorry you didn't like my book, Norman," I told him quietly. "You have delivered a body blow to my morale as a writer," and I smiled.

Mailer looked at me grumpily and glanced at the Baldwin brothers. He was obviously disappointed to find they weren't listening but were exchanging good-byes with some of the other guests. "You don't seem to be very upset," he grunted at me, losing interest. There was no time for any more anyway, because the others were already walking out to the limousine, enthusiastically waved off by our host and hostess, who must have felt as weary as referees after a fifteen-round world championship fight. But this had been even more taxing than that, for everything had been beneath the surface. It had been an existential encounter in every way; Zen masters might have

189

appreciated its underground subtleties, but I for one drove away from there with an enormous sense of disappointment, of a missed opportunity. I didn't know what the others were thinking; a heavy silence filled the limousine as it sped down the dark suburban roads back to the city. Baldwin was crunched up in a corner, his face hidden. At last he spoke. "Norman and I don't seem to have much to say to each other these days."

"The trouble is," I said, unable to resist it, "you and he have *too* much to say to each other."

And, I added to myself, for having missed one argument, there was no point in getting into another, *you and Mailer are now ducking it like everybody else.*

POSTSCRIPT
OTHER TIMES, OTHER ROLES:
THE CHAMELEON AND THE LEOPARD

The sixties now seem like an entire decade of missed opportunities and so that incident looms large and symbolically in my memory. Memories play tricks, and one trick mine plays now is to make it seem as if everything began to go to pieces or to slow down and back up after that. Everything did, but not because the two advance men weren't communicating; they merely symbolized what was happening generally. What Langston Hughes had forecast was beginning to happen: the blacks had been fashionable for a time and were now going out of fashion again. The country, after allowing itself to go through some changes, was settling down again, a little scared of the disruption that changes bring.

Bobby Kennedy, who seemed after all to have learned the lesson the Baldwin group had tried to teach him and had made an effort to get out there, had been killed in one of those mysteriously convenient assassinations. From playing hard to get, unlike many other white intellectuals, Mailer had begun to express some qualified approval of JFK's younger brother in his pursuit of the presidency. "I vote for the active principle," Mailer said. "To vote for a man who is neuter is to vote for the plague. I would rather vote for a man on the assumption he is a hero and have him turn into a monster than vote for a man who can never be a hero . . ." Now Mailer would never know what Bobby could turn into; he was unfinished, a promise without fulfillment, like his brother, JFK. Mailer must have thought the white side was cursed, indeed; even when they threw up a leader you dared face the blacks with, he didn't last long enough to be tested, to become a winner.

When Mailer heard the news that Bobby had been shot but was still alive, he bellowed "with an ugliness and pain reminiscent to his ear of the wild grunts of a wounded pig." He prayed to God to spare Kennedy's life, offering in exchange to forego some of his pleasure. The older he grew, the more religious he seemed to become. He believed "a universe in which at stricken moments one could speak quietly to whichever manifest of God or Devil was near, had to be as reasonable a philosophical proposition as any assumption that such dialogues were deluded . . ." But then the news came through his offer hadn't been accepted—Kennedy had died—and "like everybody else" he found that "he loved Bobby Kennedy by five times more in death than life." At the Democratic convention in Chicago, where Kennedy had hoped against odds to win the nomination, Mailer seemed suddenly lost, looking in vain for a replacement for RFK. As he reported in *Miami and the Siege of Chicago,* he met Eugene McCarthy, Kennedy's forerunner against Vietnam months before, and found him no successor. McCarthy seemed more like the dean of the finest English department in the land: "There wasn't that sense of a man with vast ambition and sufficient character to make it luminous, so there was not that charisma which leaves no argument about the nature of the attempt." He commented, too, that Negroes had never been charmed by McCarthy. "The Blacks did not want Whitey at his best and boniest in a year when they were out to find every justification (they were not hard to find) to hate the Honkie. But if the Black militant and the Black workingman would find no comfort or attraction in McCarthy, think then of how the Black Mixer-dixer was going to look on Clean Gene . . ." The blacks, Mailer reported, were more enthusiastic about Hubert Humphrey, particularly "every Negro on the take"—"If Hubie got in, the after-hours joints would prosper, the politics of joy would never demand that all the bars be dead by four—who could argue with that?"

But Mailer found Humphrey, even though he was nominated and was officially the winner, even less of a worthy successor to Kennedy than McCarthy. And the battle in the streets between the New Generation and the Establishment, represented by the club-swinging Chicago police, didn't involve him the way the march on the Pentagon in Washington, D.C., had done. And being Mailer, it worried him; he searched his mind for the reasons for his lack of involvement in case he was slowing up and allowing the occupational fear of the successful—that one might lose all that one had won— to dictate his actions. Unlike Baldwin, who readily confessed his fears, Mailer still seemed to think that any kind of fear was a near-mortal weakness. "It seemed to him that he had been afraid all his life, but in recent years, or so it seemed, he had learned how to take a step into his fear, how to take the action which frightened him most (and so could free him the most). He did not do it always, who could? but he had come to think that the secret to growth was to be brave a little more than one was cowardly; simple as that. Indeed why should life not be just so simple that the unlettered and untrained might also have their natural chance? It was a working philosophy and he had tried to follow it, but it seemed to him that he was deserting his own knowledge in these hours. Had his courage eroded more than his knowledge of fear the last few days? He continued to drink . . ."

He saw himself at forty-five having lost a sense of where his loyalties belonged—"to the revolution or to the stability of the country"; he felt like an anguished European intellectual of the thirties. Looking at Mailer at this unsettled stage of his life, one realized how much easier it was for a self-questioning man to find his true identity if he was black rather than white. Baldwin still had a settled role whether he liked it or not, whereas perhaps Mailer's impression of being a chameleon was merely

193

a white man's restless search for an identity that was not distorted by guilt.

Being Mailer, of course, he wasn't satisfied just to brood. Fearful he might be, he was soon seeking out an audience. Addressing a crowd that had been tear-gassed not long before, following Jean Genêt and William Burroughs as speaker—how could he resist competing with fellow writers? Mailer was cheered and a young black even held up his arm high with his own—"Black and white arms together in the air, he had been given a blessing by this Black, and felt rueful at unkind thoughts of late." He felt good, an activist again, and he had been honest with the young crowd in telling them he was leaving the field of battle to prepare for the work he did best. "Write good, baby," they cried back at him—but guilt and thoughts of fear returned when the crowd was violently attacked. "A massacre," Mailer called it, three hours later, when he was comfortable and safe. He went back to make his confession to the crowd and again they received him politely, "as if a manifest of honesty in a speaker was all they had come to hear." He told them they were revolutionary youth who had turned themselves into soldiers—they had had the courage to live at war for four days in a city that was run by "a beast." We also had a president, LBJ, who was a giant who had ended as a beast; there was a "beastiness" in the marrow of the century. Hadn't he even confessed to a "beast" in him?

Mailer was stirred up enough by the atmosphere and his reception to make one of his offers, not to God this time, or to the Devil, even, but to delegates at the convention. He would march on the convention if he could find three hundred delegates to march with him. Such a group of delegates might even scare off the Chicago police from attacking again. He and the young crowd exchanged jokes—he even got in a quotation from Voltaire—and he felt the same sense of identification Baldwin must feel with young blacks. These descendants of the White Negroes were his people! If it came to civil war, he had discovered a side he could join. Next day he ran all over town trying to raise the three hundred delegates, but everything

194

seemed to be against him, including lack of sleep and liquor "now beautifully metabolized"—"he was in that kind of unhappy shape on which comedy is built." He could "put nothing together at all" and went back, hours late, to report his failure to the young crowd. He discovered they had marched already, without him.

Once more Mailer had given himself a hero's role and had been disappointed; he had to go back to his dreams. The greatest moment at the convention was not the discovery of a fitting successor to Bobby Kennedy; it was a movie about Kennedy, good enough to make him recall his last meeting with Kennedy, in which he had tried to persuade him to take McCarthy as his running mate—"how effective two Irish Catholics would be on the same ticket, for if there were conservative Irishmen who could vote against one of them, where was the Irish Catholic in America who could vote against two?" There spoke Sergius O'Shaugnessy, but Bobby hadn't been impressed. "I wonder why you don't support Senator McCarthy. He seems more like your sort of guy, Mr. Mailer." Mailer denied it, insisting he was a Kennedy supporter. In his memory, he found Bobby "as attractive as a movie star," with gentle, beautiful eyes. How different was his impression from Baldwin's, and one wondered if Baldwin now thought more kindly of Kennedy—since he had, in effect, taken Baldwin's advice and gotten killed for his pains!

Perhaps it was this heady memory, but Mailer took one more look at the scene of battle and was seized by soldiers who passed him over to the police. Chicago Irish cops. At once "into his voice went a hint of genteel Irish 'r'." Mailer and a commander—"God save us from honest men was the expression in his eye"—got on like fellow Irishmen, the commander remembering the bad language in *The Naked and the Dead.* No charges were preferred and Mailer walked away a free man; he had managed a small victory after all. But he got into another fight and was seized again; this time the commander was "significantly less friendly." Mailer felt the cops' hatred and was pleased to find that he felt scared but ready: "he was going to try to do his best when they started to work." He felt "as electric and crazy as the cops." Why, the commander asked him severely, "do you always get into trouble?" He added that Mailer had a reputation for liking to get arrested.

Mailer protested that newspapers lied—"Look what they say about you fellows." Happiness came into the commander's face, according to Mailer, and he said, "I got to read one of your books." The commander had turned friendly after receiving a phone call—"some word must have come down," Mailer concluded. Was it the ghost of Sam Goldwyn using his influence, as gossip once had him doing in the stabbing incident? Or was it merely Mailer's fame that had made the local politicians cautious enough to call off the cops? At least in Mailer's account in *Miami and the Siege of Chicago,* the commander sounds like Sonny Liston—or a stock character in a Mailer real-life scenario.

Mailer went away from Chicago deciding he wouldn't vote for anyone—the choice of the two main parties was Nixon and Humphrey—unless he went with Eldridge Cleaver, who had announced himself as a Panther candidate. "Eldridge at least was there to know that the barricades were building across the street from the camps of barbed wire where the conscience of the world might yet be canned." Cleaver had once given his vote to Mailer instead of to Baldwin; such allegiance from a black deserved some recognition and reward.

Mailer's feeling about Bobby Kennedy was reflected in Baldwin's about Martin Luther King. Just as Mailer had once been cold to Kennedy, so Baldwin had taken a long time to warm up to King. But King, like Kennedy, had been changed by events. From being a black leader whom white politicians tried to turn into an Uncle Tom—how harmless his message of non-violence seemed to them in the face of the aggression of the Muslims and Snick and the Panthers!—Martin Luther King had become a controversial figure, a leader who was beginning to scare the very people who had felt safe with him. Day after day, he went out in obvious danger, doggedly preaching against racism and the Vietnam War. Baldwin had been much more of an admirer of Malcolm X than of Martin, but slowly he had come to admire the man's tenacity, his willingness to learn and change, all that lay beneath the minister trappings with which Baldwin was so familiar and which he found unattractive. He ended with almost a feeling of affection for him as they shared more platforms together—dear, obstinate, square, unrelenting Martin, who had survived for so long you expected he would be safe now to grow old. If they killed him, the apostle of nonviolence, they were capable of *anything,* even killing you. For that reason alone, the assassination of King would have moved Baldwin deeply, but in fact he was shattered by it. He had been feeling depressed because, against all advice, he had accepted a Hollywood offer to adapt Malcolm X's autobiography, and he was already discovering that he had made a mistake: nobody in conservative Hollywood was going to put a life as radical as Malcolm's on the screen; he was battling in vain. He was low then, feeling beaten, his imagination still reliving Malcolm's murder, when the news came that the impossible had happened—Martin, dear, obstinate, square, unrelenting Martin had got it at last and anything now was possible.

Malcolm, now Martin . . . was he next? It seemed more than a possibility at that crazy time—the course of American political life, apparently, was no longer to be decided by elections but by the gun. Well, Baldwin wouldn't wait around to be the next one to go; he wouldn't give them that satisfaction. His pendulum life, swinging between Europe and home, would change hereafter, and he would come home only for visits. He told me, "I had hoped to stop my wandering, but I can't find any real rest at home now. It's a battle all the time if you're aware of what's happening, and it wears you out. After a month at home, I begin to feel like an old man. You can't survive that way. Martin didn't. He had to live with fear all the time, every day. But I intend to survive and get my work done. They're not going to stop me!" He was intense and dramatic and incredibly nervous, verging at times on near hysteria—had Martin's murder and his conviction that he might be next cracked his self-control?

He went down to Atlanta to King's funeral in the same state of mind; it is reflected in his account in *No Name in the Street*. Like many people who had seen King at work, and knew the dues he paid, I thought that his was one public funeral where there should have been no reserved seats, particularly for public figures and politicians, most of whom merely obstructed King in life. His true mourners were the loyal nameless in the streets. *No Name in the Street* didn't describe these people; instead, Baldwin told how he came to Atlanta "incognito" and therefore couldn't get in the church until he was recognized, and then when he was settled among the privileged, he looked around and noted the other celebrities—Eartha Kitt, Marlon Brando (who had befriended the Panthers), Sidney Poitier, and so on. Oh, come on, Jimmy Baldwin, I felt like crying, don't you of all people play that celebrity game with us. Status is at the heart of racism, and what is that but just another aspect of it? Yet Baldwin—like Mailer—was such a crafty raiser of people's consciousness that one hesitated in the very act of criticizing him, in case one had missed his subtle point. Baldwin's weaknesses, like Mailer's, had a habit of becoming his strengths. He put it bluntly in *No Name in the Street:* "What in the world was I by now but an aging, lonely, sexually dubious, politically outrageous, unspeakably erratic freak?" He was challenging people to meet him on a level where there was no hiding, no pretense, no retiring behind a respectable image. Mailer did the same. But why didn't they challenge each other that way instead of ducking any head-on confrontation?

When Baldwin came to have a confrontation or rather a polite dialogue with a white spokesman, it wasn't with Mailer but with Margaret Mead, the anthropologist. This was comparatively easy for him; Dr. Mead's experience hadn't been at extremes but in comparative safety within an academic discipline, and therefore she couldn't present the same challenge as Mailer; Dr. Mead was also of an older generation and a woman —any difference of opinion was bound to be polite and not dangerously probing. A transcript of their exchange was edited and published as *A Rap on Race* by Lippincott.

"Mead: Some psychologists were doing a study somewhere, and they asked the little white boys which they would rather be, little white girls or little Negro boys. What do you think they said?

"Baldwin: I can't guess.

"Mead: They said they would rather be little Negro boys.

"Baldwin: Ha, that's encouraging. They had some sanity left . . ."

He also had an exchange with one of the younger black writers, Nikki Giovanni; how careful he was with the younger blacks, as if expecting them to treat him with the tough directness he had shown his black elders. In this conversation—which Lippincott published as *A Dialogue*—he also made a crack at Mailer's competitive attitudes, which again suggested what a great exchange they could have had if they hadn't spent the sixties avoiding it.

"Giovanni: People really feel the need to feel better than somebody, don't they?

"Baldwin: I don't know why, but they do. Being in competition with somebody is something I never understood. In my own life, I've been in competition with me . . ."

That was in one mood; in another, he would be competing with every writer on the block.

Mailer also continued to debate with other people, but people who were also easy for him, not challenging him where it really hurt. He also seemed to give more and more formal interviews to handpicked, friendly reporters for magazines like *Playboy* that he judged were read by his supporters. It came as no surprise, then, that he had decided the time was finally here—he had worked himself sufficiently back into the fold—to enter politics professionally and run for mayor of New York. He felt he was as ready as he would ever be. He was even a much more practiced public speaker. The first time he had decided to run in 1960 "on the excitements of the Kennedy candidacy and other excitements [much marijuana for one]," he had produced a maiden speech that was "private, personal, tortured in metaphor, sublimely indifferent to issues, platform,

199

or any recognizable paraphernalia of the political process, and delivered in much too rapid a voice to the assembled bewilderment of his audience, a collective (and by the end very numb) stiff clavicle of Jewish Central Park West matrons." Eugene McCarthy, one of the other speakers, had told him, "Better learn how to breathe, boy." Well, in the intervening eight years, he'd learned not only how to breathe while making a speech, but also a lot of other political tricks as well. He was ready now, but this time he wouldn't stand as a loner, an existential candidate; he would enter the competition for the Democratic Party's nomination.

He had even assembled an organization. His campaign manager was Joe Flaherty, a fellow writer. In his book *Managing Mailer,* published by Coward-McCann, Flaherty described how, before deciding to run in 1968, Mailer's team discussed whether Mailer was eligible to run for office, since years before he had stabbed his wife "and even though he'd received a suspended sentence he was in the eyes of the law a convicted felon." They decided they'd best check into the election law before they made any formal statement of candidacy to the press. They checked and found the way was legally clear, although no one could estimate how much that old scandal might dog the candidate—it was a skeleton in Mailer's closet comparable to the Chappaquiddick incident in Teddy Kennedy's. I only realized this when I was in a large bookstore at a time one of Mailer's books was published and I heard the bookstore manager telling someone she would never forgive Norman for stabbing his wife. The mistake he had probably made—like Teddy Kennedy—was not to come out with an exhaustive statement immediately afterward; what a subject it would have been for one of his long, brilliant essays!

He chose as his running mate—for president of the City Council—Jimmy Breslin, the writer and resident New York City "police station genius," as Philip Roth called him. Breslin was the kind of Irish-American Mailer had once seemed to be; the two running mates, side-by-side, mutually congratulatory, seemed oddly related, almost like opposite extremes of the same person, each containing something of what the other would have liked to have been.

Early on in the campaign, Mailer's campaign manager discovered that Mailer "had a one-way love affair with street types. If someone had been part of an experience foreign to his own (being black, a convict, a prizefighter), Mailer found in him occult powers bestowed only on the children of the gutters. Their dreariness of thought and total lack of performance in any function assigned to them made no difference to him. This enchantment had to do with Mailer's high sense of intrigue and his romantic notion of the streets. That the gutter was a spawning ground which produced dullness far more often than genius was never considered. It was a characteristic I found unattractive, similar to that of society broads who chase saxophone players and bouncers . . ."

If blacks, even the most casual street types, seemed to have occult powers, we catch a glimpse then of how dangerous the brilliant Baldwin must have appeared. Flo Kennedy, a black lawyer and confidante of the Panthers, had early on warned the candidate: "Norman, you don't know a goddamn thing about the blacks," to which Mailer countered with what his campaign manager called a satanic grin: "Flo, darling, to know one is to fuck one." Oh, what an opening that would have given Ali-Baldwin! Boom, and the candidate would have been mentally on his back.

I watched him campaigning in the streets of New York, his mop of curly graying hair trimmed to executive length, wearing a sober suit; he looked every inch the man of respectability, but when he talked, he seemed unsure of whether he was a politician, solid and worthy of your vote, or an intellectual and literary celebrity. He brought up all his pet themes—New York became the plague in a teacup, as concentrated as it could be. The danger was that The Beast in him he'd described in *The Armies of the Night* was capable of taking over the candidate, and he seemed to do just that at a meeting at the Village Gate. Glass in hand, imitating a Southern sheriff, Mailer abused his supporters and was the subject of a mocking report in the

201

highly respectable *New York Times* next day; all over town pro politicians were shaking their heads and saying, "What did I tell you?"

Mailer, however, proved himself a much better and much more industrious candidate than anybody expected, and although he and Breslin lost by a landslide in the Democratic Primary—they were fourth out of five—he had the satisfaction of both fulfilling an ambition and dramatizing his whole philosophy of life. And his political ambitions obviously were still very much alive. When he appeared as a defense witness in the trial of the Chicago 7, this dialogue occurred:

"Mailer: I ran in the Democratic Primary for mayor last spring, and I came in fourth in a field of five.

"The Court: "You didn't say what city, sir.

"Mailer: I am sorry, Judge, in New York City.

"The Court: I knew I haven't seen your name on our ballot.

"Mailer: It is my deep desire, Judge, to run for mayor in Chicago . . ."

The Chicago 7 were among the leaders of the street demonstrations at the time of the convention, and to Mailer, they must have appeared—particularly Abbie Hoffman and Jerry Rubin—like leading sons of White Negroes. Yet there were differences. Abbie Hoffman told the judge they were alienated young people who resided in Woodstock Nation, which was "dedicated to cooperation versus competition." Asked his age, Hoffman said he was thirty-three, a child of the sixties. When was he born? "Psychologically, 1960." Mailer, who, when asked to stick to the point in his answers, said, "I have been exposed to the world as a man possessed of a rambling mind," came to defend his children. When asked if Jerry Rubin used the word "intimidate," Mailer replied: "I use the word 'intimidate' because possibly since I am a bully by nature, unlike anyone else in this court, I tend to think in terms of intimidation, but I don't think Mr. Rubin does. He thinks in terms of cataclysm, of having people become aroused, to reveal their guilt, their own evil, if you will . . ."

But these descendants of Mailer's White Negroes were to

endure as an influence no more than their black equivalents had in the face of official harassment. As the sixties turned into the seventies, the names of the Chicago 7 began to slip back into obscurity. Jerry Rubin and Abbie Hoffman showed up at the next conventions, but it was four years later, and their parodies and mad satire had lost most of their political power; now they seemed to most of their audience to be mere eccentrics. This time they came not as subjects of the media but as part of it, for both of them were writing books and had media passes. "I'm having an identity crisis," Mailer reported Rubin as saying "with his broad smile which welcomes all human phenomena including upheavals in himself."

Rubin was not the only one having an identity crisis. Mailer noted, for example, "a Black Jew"—ah, Baldwin and Mailer combined!—who "sings for the young, does imitations for the old and has turned from Democrat to Republican." That was presumably Sammy Davis, Jr. And Mailer went on to a reception given by other blacks supporting Nixon. "Negro doctors, lawyers, and businessmen, delegates most of them, move around with their wives who are heavyset. There is not a jive Black in sight, no smocks, sarongs, or flaring Afros. No prime evil. Nothing carnal. The mood, if boring, is absolutely safe." And Mailer comments of himself: "He has not felt so safe among Blacks in years. The spirit is sullen, long-suffering and secure. It is as if he has been invited to a gathering of pullman porters." Then some young blacks entered—"They are saltier in their stance for they are self-defensive. Still, there is no menace. Just safety. Will America be miserable when the streets are safe?"

Perhaps Mailer, too, was changing, if not having an identity crisis, for he seemed far less interested now in active politics than in developing his role as a Voyeur Reporter, covering everything from the astronauts' trip to the moon to the cult of the late Marilyn Monroe and the advent of Women's Liberation. The old Harvard student of aeronautical engineering reappeared in him when he wrote about the moonshot. He relished trying to make simple sense of the technical details and transform them into readable prose—and trying to make the astronauts (and the moon) into part of the Mailer scene. Again he made himself a character in the action, though there were limitations this time on how far he could go and they clearly limited his book. He needed to be up there on the moon to describe the landing firsthand, but that was impossible, so his account at the most important point had a secondhand quality; it was as though in *The Armies of the Night* he'd only described the arrest of other people and what they had told him about how they were treated in jail; how that would have weakened the power of what he had to say!

"If we approach our subject via Aquarius," he wrote in *Of a Fire on the Moon,* "it is because he is a detective of sorts, and different in spirit from eight years ago. He has learned to live with questions . . ." He had been discussing the suicide of Hemingway that took place eight years previously—"Now the greatest living romantic was dead. Dread was loose . . ."—but it might also have been that stabbing incident just before; that, too, must have taught him to live without easy answers. The astronauts he saw as the core of some magnetic human force called "Americanism, Protestantism, or Waspitude"; they were the knights of the silent majority. God or Devil at the helm— that was the question behind the trip, and it was Mailer's profession "to live alone with thoughts at the very edge of his mental reach." Once he had thought of extreme experience in physical terms; now the "very edge" was mental. With Vietnam condemned by a majority and the politicians therefore forced to put an end to the war, landing on the moon was now a more challenging subject for Mailer's brooding. Vietnam had been a scientific war; this was a scientific exploration—an important consideration for a man who believed science was the last of the religions human beings truly believed in.

Damn the blacks who thought the moon, like Vietnam, was just another attempt to distract attention from their cause— that was too parochial a thought for Aquarius. He had even digested Nixon now, for Nixon as a loser was one thing, but as a winner he was another, requiring more thought. When Mailer had covered the Republican Convention that nominated Nixon for president for a second time, he was in a sour enough mood to appreciate the occasion. A knight of Waspitude could not have been more testy about the blacks (Was this the same man who had written *The White Negro?*), for he complained: ". . . the reporter became aware after a while of a curious emotion in himself, for he had not ever felt it consciously before —it was a simple emotion and very unpleasant to him—he was getting tired of Negroes and their rights. It was a miserable recognition, and on many a count, for if he felt even a hint this way, then what immeasurable tides of rage must be loose in America itself? . . ."

And then there was this: ". . . over the last ten years if he had had fifty friendships with Negroes sufficiently true to engage a part of his heart, then was it ten or even five of those fifty which had turned out well? Aware of his own egocentricity, his ability to justify his own actions through many a strait gate, still it seemed to him that for the most part, putting color to the side—if indeed that were ever permissible—the fault, man to man, had been his less often, that he had looked through the catechism of every liberal excuse, had adopted the blame, been ready to give blessing and forgive, and had succeeded merely in deadening the generosity of his heart. Or was he stingier than he dreamed, more lacking in the true if exorbitant demand for compassion without measure, was the black liberty to exploit the white man without measure, which he had claimed for the black so often, 'If I were a Negro, I'd exploit everything in sight,' was this black liberty he had so freely offered finally too offensive for him to support? He was weary to the bone of listening to black cries of black superiority in sex, black superiority in beauty, black superiority in war . . ."

Perhaps, as he admitted himself, he had become, over the dues-paying years, more conservative than he had realized, a closet Republican—though I suspect a little of it was still the old chameleon writer taking on the color of any scene he was describing. When Nixon, then president, an unbelievable circumstance only a few years before, gave a dinner party for the crew of Apollo II, Mailer commented: "If Aquarius thought Nixon's most striking effect upon America was as a bloodletter who would reduce all passions, Aquarius was on the other hand not so certain that America had not needed a leech for its fever. From across a political divide, he admired what he had come to decide was Nixon's grasp on political genius—to be so unpopular and yet successful—that was genius! So Aquarius was bored with liberals who thought politics was equal to loathing Nixon . . ."

I wondered what Baldwin would make of it all. To find a reason for scampering back to Europe, he needn't have listened to the declared racists but could have despaired over the way many of the civil rights movement's former friends were talking. Some of the celebrities, white and black, who had raised funds for Martin Luther King and the Kennedys had switched full circle and now supported Richard Nixon. I saw Baldwin briefly at a family Christmas party; he didn't even want to talk about it. Of course, he said, the civil rights movement had died with Martin; the dreams had all died with him, the hope of some kind of peaceful revolution that would really change our attitudes and and the way we lived.

"At least all the hatreds, the hostility, have come out in the open," I said. "The relationship is equal now."

Baldwin shrugged; he was really past talking about it. He had a house in the south of France; he was flying back there in the morning. One good piece of news was that Tony Maynard had at last got out of prison; he was now officially innocent and free, fulfilling his dream of lying on a beach somewhere. It was as though we were back in the Eisenhower fifties; everybody was going his own way—in the last presidential election, nearly half the voters hadn't bothered to cast a ballot.

Mailer made another movie, on Long Island; he got a lot of publicity playing the role of Norman Mailer, Movie Actor and Director, and wrote a long essay about his theory of moviemaking. He also turned up as a character in a novel, *American Mischief* by Alan Lelchuk (published by Farrar, Straus, and Giroux). According to *The New York Times,* he was very annoyed about it—perhaps because he was killed in the novel. Lelchuk made him sound like a tough-talking caricature of the old bantam-cock movie actor, James Cagney. " 'Now put the rod away,' he began, delivering the Cagney-noun out of the corner of his mouth, inhaling deeply, a brilliant melodramatist to the end." And the end comes swiftly but in a way that probably enraged Mailer: "I took two steps forward, leaned behind him, and placed the .38 at his anus . . ." The justification for Mailer's murder in the novel was that it was carrying Mailer's own ideas into practice, proof of how seriously his bold thinking (in such books as *An American Dream*) was being taken. It seemed to me a good joke—a reader taking a writer *too* seriously—but Mailer apparently wasn't amused.

I wondered if he was amused by what was happening to Nixon. Re-elected by a landslide, the newspapers said, though in reality it was by a minority of the voters, since even fewer than usual had voted, Nixon was now sinking his whole administration into the quicksands that became known as Watergate. The winner was rapidly becoming an all-time loser; might Baldwin now justifiably turn on Mailer and demand to know whether this was a "knight of the Silent Majority"?

Mailer turned back to boxing for relief from politics; it was certainly simpler, though trying to describe Muhammad Ali was like working your way out of a labyrinth. Mailer covered Ali's defense of his championship against George Foreman in Zaire, thus fulfilling Eldridge Cleaver's prediction about his dealing with Africa; through Ali, he seemed to be trying to recover some of the ground he'd lost over Nixon. Ali, the World's Greatest Athlete, was "in danger of being our most beautiful man." Mailer even found allies among American blacks against the arrogance of Africans: "Manners became so bad that American blacks were snarling at African blacks . . ." He was introduced by Ali as "a man of wisdom" —Ah, who could be sure that that wasn't the mythical "Negro irony"?—and Foreman described him as "the champ among writers." Mailer congratulated himself that "these days Norman was being welcomed by Blacks." It bewildered him a little for he hadn't earned it by his writing half as much as he might have ten or fifteen years earlier. He gathered he had made an impression, because a story had gone out that he was to get a million for his next novel; big exaggeration, and how much would he keep with five wives and seven children, but what did it matter out there in Africa? He was getting the same kind of money for just writing that normally only the Alis collected! His stock shot up. "Once, he would have been miserable at being able to prosper from such values. But his love affair with the Black soul, a sentimental orgy at its worst, had been given a drubbing through the seasons of Black Power. He no longer knew whether he loved Blacks or secretly disliked them, which had to be the dirtiest secret in his American life . . ."

He was turning against all that he had found to praise in *The White Negro;* perhaps now he would understand why it had earned Baldwin's fury and Cleaver's praise. "So much resentment had developed for black style, black snobbery, black rhetoric, black pimps, superfly, and all that virtuoso handling of the ho. The pride Blacks took in their skill as pimps! . . ." Which blacks? He was still responding to the street-life infatuation that had disturbed his campaign manager, not to mention Baldwin, who had tried to show him that blacks were as complicated and many-layered as whites. Yet feeling this way, the old chameleon could still find himself in Africa. Reading a book on *Bantu Philosophy,* "he discovered that the instinctive philosophy of African tribesmen happened to be close to his own," he wrote in *The Fight.* "Bantu philosophy, he soon learned, saw humans as forces, not beings. Without putting it into words, he had always believed that. It gave a powerful shift to his thoughts . . ."

He also made the cover of *Time* at last—but he had to share it with the late Marilyn Monroe whose biography, or psychohistory, he had written. Although he had never met her, he made her a part of the Mailer story; once more the voyeur found a way into the action. His secret ambition had been to steal Marilyn from his fellow Jewish writer, Arthur Miller, who was then married to her. The competitor, even in marriage! "In all his vanity he thought no one was so well suited to bring out the best in her as himself, a conceit which fifty million other men may also have held." It was only a few marriages—"a few failures"—later that "he could recognize how he would have done no better than Miller and probably have been damaged further in the process." *Time* suggested that *The Naked and the Dead* would have been the perfect title for his Marilyn book. It described Mailer as "The Grand Middle-Aged Man of American Letters," extremely sensitive to criticism, a reconciliation of opposites, a radical conservative, a combination of street toughness and book learning. Every Mailer book was "a trip with Virgil through the underground." The magazine quoted Mailer as saying, "If we're going to come of age, we've got to stop this piety toward our leaders," and then commented editorially: "That piety must include the homage shown to literary as well as political and film stars. Perhaps Norman Mailer has been treated too piously; maybe he has been on top too long."

A sly dig at the winner, but then Mailer had taken his own dig at *Time;* at best it was still an uneasy relationship. In *The Prisoner of Sex,* Mailer recalled the time when the magazine "solemnly took him out in the backyard every few weeks to give him a going-over" and he had struck back by capturing "the mistress of a potentate of *Time*"—an experience, he wrote, that marked him "profoundly (to a marriage and one of his children indeed!)" and he was "never again so good a revolutionary—in fact, he ended as a Left Conservative." The potentate, however, was long since gone and Mailer and the present editor of *Time* "had become cordial yet wary." It was vague, but gossip filled in the names.

There were rumors of a Nobel Prize which Mailer made much of, finally deciding he didn't want it, not that year, that season "of large and little deaths for ten thousand seedlings of the psyche." He and his wife had parted after nearly seven years—"What monstrous timing it would be to win a prize now and smile one's mouth out over a choppy sea of congratulations," he wrote in *The Prisoner of Sex.* He needn't have wor-

209

ried. He was soon out of the race and it was then between his old hero, André Malraux, and Samuel Beckett, with the solitary, uncompetitive Irishman the eventual winner over the French politician-adventurer-novelist.

He took on Women's Liberation in *The Prisoner of Sex;* some women accused him of condescending to them; others said he was an unrepentant male chauvinist; in truth, Women's Lib seemed to annoy him as much as the blacks. "He could love a woman and she might even sprain her back before a hundred sinks of dishes in a month, but he would not be happy to help her if his work should suffer, no, not unless her work was as valuable as his own . . ."

He celebrated his fiftieth birthday with a public party at which he called for an organization to investigate the FBI and the CIA (surely Baldwin would have agreed with that!). His sense of when an idea was fashionable was as acute as ever . . . when he took up blacks again in a big way, one would know their time had come again. Until then, he was likely to be off in any direction, Mailerizing anything that came up. There was something both exasperating and exemplary in his muscling in on every new controversy, his eagerness to find new winners; yet what peaks beyond his present reach he might be able to scale if he was willing to side with the losers! The way he was going now would take him and Baldwin further and further apart.

I saw him on TV with Muhammad Ali; graying and benign, he looked like a plumpish rabbi as he exchanged self-conscious jokes with a super-confident Ali, trim at fighting weight. But the rabbinical resemblance didn't seem to be by design; Mailer still wasn't running as a Jew. As Philip Roth pointed out in *Reading Myself and Others:* "Jewish cultural audiences, which are generally pleased to hear Saul Bellow and Bernard Malamud identified by critics as Jewish writers, are perfectly content that by and large Norman Mailer, with all his considerable influence and stature, should go forth onto the lecture platform and the television talk shows as a writer, *period.* This is obviously okay too with the author of *The Deer Park* and *An*

210

American Dream, to name just two of his books with heroes he chooses not to call Cohen . . ." One suspects, however, that many Jews, particularly of the more militant younger generation, are proud of Mailer as an older Jew who would not allow himself to be discriminated against without attacking back.

I met Mailer not long after his exchange with Ali—in the flesh this time, not on the TV screen—how distant he seemed even face-to-face after the TV close-ups. He didn't look at all rabbinical as he circulated, beaming politely, joking, chuckling, through the crowd at a reception for Gregory Hemingway, who had written a book about his father, *Papa: A Personal Memoir.* Mailer had contributed a preface, almost paternal in tone (". . . it is unlike most books written by sons about great fathers. There is nothing slavish here . . ."), sounding almost like a stand-in for Papa himself, even though Papa was quoted in the book as saying, "Mailer's probably the best postwar writer. He's a psycho, but the psycho part is the most interesting thing about him . . ." That couldn't have pleased Mailer.

Standing beside Gregory Hemingway, there seemed even to be a family resemblance: both men were stocky, aggressive, and nervously hearty. Mailer was already talking—as Papa did in later life—of the Big Novel he was writing; Mailer was tempting fate, because Papa had never finished his. Mailer beamed as Gregory Hemingway, a doctor by profession, said modestly, "I've just used my memory in my book—unlike a real professional writer like you, Norman, who uses his imagination." That, anyway, seemed to please him.

Across the Hemingway African Museum in New York, where the reception was being held, a black journalist gazed at Mailer as if Mailer's mere appearance created a challenge, and worked himself up, saying, "Mailer and his macho remind me of a lower-class black stud after he's taken off his dungarees . . ." Had Mailer come all this way to be mistaken for—not an Irishman any longer, but a black? How would he take *that?* I mentioned Baldwin, and the black journalist said Jimmy didn't have Norman's macho hang-ups—they were Tweedledum and Tweedledee. I found myself defending Mailer and his talent, his brave, imaginative trips here, there, and everywhere (though no longer to extremes). The black journalist made me think I might have been too hard on Mailer. I had never seen him relaxing with his family, as I had seen Baldwin. Whites could be too hard on whites, and sometimes took each other's familiar qualities too much for granted. An irony of the color line was that sometimes it was easier to appreciate the virtues of the other side. But of course there was no "other side." Mailer and Baldwin were on the same side: that was the real irony.

Baldwin came back from the south of France for a visit. I hadn't seen him for a long time when unexpectedly I bumped into him on Broadway, near his mother's home. He, too, was over fifty now. His hair wasn't as black and he seemed quieter, more detached, as if he was determined not to get angry about anything. A French friend was with him, and back at his apartment, there were several black women writers talking among themselves like a Shakespearean chorus, and Tony Maynard's sister, Valerie, was also there. Baldwin's last novel, *If Beale Street Could Talk,* reflected some of his experiences in the Maynard case; it was a simple love story about a woman whose man goes to prison—those prison visits had marked Baldwin.

His old movie ambitions had also found their way into another book, *The Devil Finds Work,* but it was very different from Mailer's movie essays. Where Mailer laid down a philosophy of movie-making, Baldwin related movies to the black experience. In that sense he hadn't changed, and inevitably he was criticized for it; some saw him still expressing attitudes that were fresh in the sixties but which they considered old-fashioned in the seventies. He didn't challenge new intellectual fashions the way Mailer did; if Mailer sometimes seemed like a chameleon, Baldwin was a leopard that didn't change his spots; he was loyal to the cause of his life, but that wasn't necessarily good for his work.

There *had* been changes, big ones. Why, even the Muslims now believed in integration. Elijah Muhammad was dead and his son, Wallace, who was his successor, not only opened the doors to whites but actively recruited them—White Muslims!

212

Eldridge Cleaver came home to face the charges against him, talking like a conservative patriot who preferred the U.S. at any price, and his old Panther comrade, Huey Newton, in temporary exile in Cuba, attacked him for it. The Panthers were no more an active force and the new generation had produced no successor. The whole picture seemed to have changed—until riots broke out among the Boston Irish over school busing, the latest attempt at enforced integration of the schools, and suddenly the calendar seemed to turn right back to the fifties. It was easy then to understand why Baldwin seemed to be still set in the same old key.

Both he and Mailer had survived longer than Scott Fitzgerald, but was it possible that their best work was already behind them, as Hemingway's and Faulkner's had been at their age? Hemingway had often worried over the fact that American writers didn't seem to have endurance, and he went on to provide yet another example of it himself. Would Mailer and Baldwin do the same—or would they have a productive old age and go the equivalent, as Mailer might say, of life's full fifteen rounds, with no early knockouts, no retirements, no failing to come out of their corners, a triumph of endurance right up to the end—was it possible?

The last time I'd seen Mailer he was just back from Rome, where the gossip columnists had him writing a movie script— a Mailer Western, one magazine reported—and rowing with the Italian producer: the wear-and-tear of earning a star's living.

The last time I saw Baldwin a magazine photographer was taking pictures all the time we were talking. His mother, upstairs, was said to be annoyed that Baldwin didn't restrict such show business sessions to business hours. Being on stage all the time like that could play hell with your sense of reality. Yet Baldwin still seemed to need the reassurance of fame, the security of being a star. In his fears, his insecurities, perhaps even in his attitude toward his own celebrity (which had become his defense against his fears), he showed that a large part of him could never overcome the effects of the environment he was

213

born into. Part of him would forever be a scared little boy in the ghetto. It was a nightmare common to Baldwin's generation. The biggest, most lasting success of the movement, it seemed now, had been to transform these fears into a deep feeling of self-confidence in the generation after Baldwin's, a deep feeling that, whatever the brainwashing to the contrary, *black is beautiful.* Baldwin and this new generation eyed each other a little suspiciously, even though they were standing on his shoulders, benefiting from his perceptions. Reputations, celebrities, meant little to them apparently: they made it clear that if some black stars they thought had sold out returned to the Apollo in Harlem, they would boo them or, as one young basketball player told me about a well-known black singer, "We'll tomato her." Baldwin wouldn't be booed, wouldn't be tomatoed, and that was still more important to him than the critics' good opinion.

We talked a little about the sixties, reminiscing as if it was all far, far back in the dim past, and about Tony Maynard and about Henry James's essays on returning to America. Baldwin was nervous, tentative, the embers of his old intense self. Maybe he was just tired. He'd been lecturing at colleges—and at some prisons: an exile trying to stay in touch.

I had been reading Tennessee Williams' *Memoirs,* and I mentioned it because Tennessee Williams had introduced me to Baldwin. Williams was a white Southerner in his sixties; he was also America's leading living playwright. A passage at the end of his memoirs confused me—I looked for a joke but couldn't find one. I could only conclude that it was supposed to be taken seriously, particularly as it referred to his beloved sister, Rose, though it seemed like such a naked example of what Lorraine Hansberry had called—in reference to Mailer—the "new paternalism." I gave it to Baldwin to read, hoping he would be able to point out some deep irony I had missed:

"Rose is fond of the blacks, as I am, perhaps because of our devotion to our beautiful black nurse Ozzie when we were children in Mississippi. She always used to conclude her letters to me with, 'Love to my children, white or black.' I noticed

214

that in New York, on the streets and in stores, Rose was continually waving to children of both races . . ."

Baldwin sighed.

Langston Hughes was still right.

ACKNOWLEDGMENTS

Although this book describes my personal experiences with Norman Mailer and James Baldwin, I have related those experiences to their works and have occasionally quoted briefly from them to underline or explain some aspect. The books I have found most helpful include:

By Mailer: *The Naked and the Dead,* first published by Rinehart; *Barbary Shore* (Rinehart); *The Deer Park* (G.P. Putnam's Sons); *Advertisements for Myself* (G.P. Putnam's Sons); *The Presidential Papers* (G.P. Putnam's Sons); *An American Dream* (The Dial Press); *Cannibals and Christians* (The Dial Press); *Why Are We in Vietnam?* (G.P. Putnam's Sons); *The Armies of the Night* (New American Library); *Miami and the Siege of Chicago* (New American Library); *Of a Fire on the Moon* (Little, Brown and Company); *The Prisoner of Sex* (Little, Brown and Company); *Maidstone: A Mystery* (New American Library); *Existential Errands* (Little, Brown and Company); *Marilyn* (Grosset & Dunlap, Inc.); *St. George and the Godfather* (New American Library); *The Fight* (Little, Brown and Company).

By Baldwin: *Go Tell It on the Mountain* (The Dial Press); *Notes of a Native Son* (Beacon Press); *Giovanni's Room* (The Dial Press); *Nobody Knows My Name* (The Dial Press); *Another Country* (The Dial Press); *The Fire Next Time* (The Dial Press); *Blues for Mr. Charlie* (The Dial Press); *Going to Meet*

216

the Man (The Dial Press); *Tell Me How Long the Train's Been Gone* (The Dial Press); *No Name in the Street* (The Dial Press); *If Beale Street Could Talk* (The Dial Press); *The Devil Finds Work* (The Dial Press).